THE TANTRIC SEX

HANDBOOK

\-

THE BEST GUIDE FOR TANTRIC HEALING AND HISTORY,

TANTRIC EXERCISES, ART, ROMANCE, DATING, AND SACRED SEX

POSITIONS FOR MEN AND WOMEN

Disclaimer

The information contained cannot be considered a substitute for treatment as prescribed by a therapist or other professional. By reading this book, you are assuming all risks associated with using the advice, data, and suggestions given below, with a full understanding that you, solely, are responsible for anything that may occur as a result of putting this information into action in any way – regardless of your interpretation of the advice.

TABLE OF CONTENTS

INTRODUCTION

Everything is certainly blissful when it comes to the word sex. However, there are heights and levels to it, are you ready to experience a mind bugging and an experience that will take you to the highest cloud leaving your body exploding with pleasure even at the lightest touch. Picture yourself being in a situation of sexual bliss where every act seems to melt inside of you because you love every pang of it. If you would like this experience, then you're reading the perfect guide! Here, you will learn everything there is to know about tantric sex, and have the knowledge of the rudiments of the pleasure so you could reach the level of a blissful moments in your sex life. The tantric practices you will learn in this eBook will also help you improve unity in your relationship and marriage. Enjoy!!!

CHAPTER ONE: WHAT IS TANTRA?

Put simply, it involves slowing down and enjoying all of the build up to the main event, rather than rushing to get there. It is certainly the opposite of a quickie; Tantric sex is all about enjoying each other and increasing intimacy. Tantric sex is an ancient Hindu practice that has been going for over 5,000 years, and means 'the weaving and expansion of energy'. Tantra traditions comes from ancient practices in Nepal, China and India which was once reserved for royalty and alas! It is here for one and for all. It is a slow form of sex that's said to increase intimacy and create a mind-body connection that can lead to powerful orgasms. Tantric sex – or Tantra as it's often known – can be done by anyone interested in rebooting their sex life and finding new depth to their love-making. If that sounds confusing, think of it this way – if quickie sex is the sexual equivalent of a takeaway, tantric sex is like your favourite meal, slowly and lovingly prepared and all the more delicious thanks to the wait. Tantra sex is a form of sexual healing that heals hurts of the past and makes you more open to love.

TANTRA AS A SPIRITUAL PATH TO INTENSE LOVE.

The variances in spiritual practices and the application of technology has enabled the tantric sex more appreciated deeper and there is more desire to satisfy sexual urges in new dimensions

THE SACREDNESS OF TANTRIC SEX

This sacred sex, as mind blowing as it is, doesn't just end in the physical way. In the sacred sex lies a powerful energy generator that does to your soul and body MAGIC! Just assume several watts of power convulsing around your sexual area which conduct your heart and brain some magic orgasms, leaving you in a state of a satisfied happiness. Tantric sex makes use of various devotional exercises and practices to fulfill its purpose One such practice is Yoga. These exercises help to awake and channel the outpouring and terrific energy within the body, rotate same energy with your partner and disperse it to the world. It is meant for personal satisfaction and shared-intimacy.

WHAT SACRED SEX IS

In order to understand Tantric sex better, we need to know what sacred sex is. Sacred sex is about the consciousness and awareness which we bring to the act, taking it from mere physical pleasure to a spiritual experience of growth, expansion and personal evolution. It refers to the combination of two individuals with the intent of a holistic union. Sacred sex is a sexual activity a couple engages in, to reach a divine union and bliss

It is important to know that it's not for personal excitement neither for lust nor to use the other person for emotional tool. The aim of Sacred sex is not for achieving lust or using the other partner for personal or sexual satisfaction. It is when a couple comes together in unison with a joint purpose and a unified goal.

Sacred sex is taken seriously and done with utmost

4

reverence. The fusion of two beings is referred to as an act of holiness which is to be done with great respect and not to be taken with levity. Sacred sex serves as a link between the physical and spiritual world and can only be accessed through a willing, connected body and breath.

There are different types of tantra that are being practiced in recent times. While some originated from ancient practices; others have changed over the years and integrated the modern western practices to make them more appealing. However, whether ancient or modern tantra, their practices are premised on similar principles. Some of these principles include

- The sacredness of sexuality
- Equality of all human beings
- The road to achieving bliss is through sexual union
- The breath is Paramount in tantra
- Belief in sexual energy channels or Chakras
- Tantra is beneficial to the individual, couple and the society.

The principles and views tantra propose is not all new and strange. Even if you don't know what it entails, it is likely that you have heard it been discussed by a friend or another person. You might have even experienced the feeling of tantra while having sex with your partner and you reached that stage of joint ecstasy. A moment in which you felt a taste of heaven and at peace with the world.

Tantric sex helps to create a deep connection between you and your partner and the universe. This might prove difficult because it means you will have to let go of your rational analytical mind. The thinking part that defines your image, your present needs and problems you think you have. Naturally your mind will kick against you giving up your worries. However, with Tantric sex, you can effectively control your mind and put a halt to your worrying

WHAT IS FREEDOM IN TANTRIC SEX?

Nothing can be used to compare the height of freedom the tantric sex gives, it frees the mind, the body and the soul. Alongside with its desired fulfillment, it does the 'trinity' work. It comes with peace of mind and erase any form of negativity as you dive to the world of shared-intimacy and personal fulfilment with your beloved. Tantric sex serves as a liberator that set the mind, body and soul free in order to enjoy the blissful and desired sexual experience. It begins with the mind when you set your mind to the blissful moment beginning from the powerful gaze of your partner, there is nowhere and nothing to hide, and you practice fully revealing yourself to the other with all that you feel and all that you are. You see them fully while at the same time letting yourself be seen.

Sit up straight on a pillow or chair facing your partner. You can look left eye to left eye or just gaze softly at both eyes, and you can also hold hands if you like. Let the love that is in your heart shine out through your eyes. Gazing at your beloved, see the divine spark in their eyes, marveling at the pure life force that is animating them. Feel the sacredness of this simple moment together.

Try for two minutes. Notice what emotions or sensations come up, or if you feel tempted to look away. It isn't a staring contest, so you can always close your eyes for a few seconds and then open them again. Here, the mind, the body and the soul get freed, a new world is formed through this divine sexual experience. It also breaks challenges, negativity, barriers, blockages from within you and between you and your beloved, this is achieved by increasing sexual acts into divine practices (which set the mind, the body and the soul free) and also making the beloved as one for whom every sensation and sexual movements does a magic to the mind, body and soul and it's considered to be a divine gift.

TANTRIC SEX AS SEXUAL HEALING

When tantric sex is described as a pathway to sexual healing, it is not related to MARVIN GAYE'S song 'SEXUAL HEALING'. In tantric sex, your partner is honoured and respected and you are taught ways to treat your partner like gods and goddesses.

Tantric Sex in terms of sexual healing is directed at attaining goals which can be achieved through releasing of your body and mind. Releasing of your body and letting go of your preconceived ideas means you are setting your body to be healed. You are free to get new states of love even outside sexual pleasure. Here the pathway of healing is being convoked. Humans (variably men and women) might have suffered hurts, and negativity from previous relationships, which create a deep wound in their sexual pleasure towards their beloved. Tantric sex is aimed at healing all kinds of pain, and making you and your beloved free and at peace with each other. While at it, it gives you the confidence to be open to love without fear or guilt of the past.

There are three popular steps involved in Tantric sex as a pathway to healing which are inscribed in the acronym 'ERR' which is explained below;

•Establishing the past hurts imagine, whether real or imagined, through sexual action and sexual devotional exercises.

•Revealing strong feelings attached to the previous hurts.

•Repairing previous hurts with positive feelings and actions.

TANTRIC SEX AS A HEALING TOOL

Coupled with the amazing benefits it offers, another

importance of tantric sex is its amazing healing power. It can be used for gradually healing the body, spirit and mind. We all experience and suffer from social and relationship ills. Irrespective of your gender-at one point in time in your life, you would have faced rejections, disappointments, and hurts from the previous relationships you have engaged in.

However Tantric sex, through its workouts and sacred rituals detailed in this eBook can be used to heal the body, and give freedom to the spirit and mind from its previously afflicted state. Tantric sex will get you feeling peaceful and sweet. It will also reconstruct your social and sexual energy to put you in a position to give and receive love. So, in place of your disappointment, you will feel accepted. In case of fear, you will feel love, in case of guilt, you will feel blameless, that is what Tantric sex can give to you.

There are three main steps you are required to carry out to heal yourself sexually with the advanced powers of tantric sex.

Firstly, you are to understand and pinpoint the hurts you got from your past relationships that are still with you. You can achieve this through sexual meditation, and stimulation.

Secondly you will release the emotions that comes accompanied with these hurts. This is important because if you still have these powerful emotions with you, you won't be able to receive new positive ones offered by Tantra.

Lastly through sexual stimulation, you will replace your previous hurts and bad emotions with positive experience and   emotions.

TANTRIC SEX: WHAT SCIENCE SAY?

Tantric sex increases the rate at which the body generates changes that are in alignment with the regular euphoric moments, which includes happy enzymes like the 'endorphins ' and 'oxytocins'. The two chemical enzymes are the major ones responsible for reactions when having sex. Tantrism is an ancient spiritual practice that focuses on sexual ritual to achieve transcendent states. It helps one calm the mind, harmonise the emotions and concentrate the spirit before intercourse. Then, having settled the body and composed one's thoughts, penetrate deeply and move slowly. Tantric sex which is a 5,000-year-old ancient Eastern spiritual practice involving an emotional and energetic connection, may help us become more intimate and reach our own sexual paradise.

CHAPTER TWO: TANTRIC SEX AND ITS ENERGY CONNECTIVITY

Tantric sex, then, may help us in achieving so much more as sexual beings, without the concept of penetration. We have been stereotyped by the society to believe sex without penetration is "merely" foreplay and nothing more. However, penetration is not an important factor for peak erotic pleasure or orgasm. "Orgasmic energies," the process of arousal that often culminates in orgasm, is a full-body experience achieved by keeping energy flowing through us smoothly and naturally. Intercourse emotionally, as well as physically, connects two people due to the release of oxytocin (the love hormone) in the brain. But it also connects them spiritually and energetically.

With tantric sex, or spiritual sex, the focus is on the energy exchanged between one spiritual being and another. The body is merely the channel. That's why it's essential to discover the energy passage in the body and help focus on having a dominant and manipulative control of the movement of that energy within the connections. The energies combination with your partner help to liquify negative feelings like separation and helps to become a union. If we apply tantra's concepts to physical intimacy, we can see how intercourse is a spiritual catalyst focusing on connection, awakening, healing and transformation. Tantric sex connects major hormones in the brain i.e. the pineal and pituitary that is equivalent and similar to energy centers like chakra. The energies you channel during tantric sex flow throughout your body and can intensify your orgasm.

WHY TANTRIC SEX IS MAGICAL

Tantric sex is not just your normal sec styles or positions. It isn't just for fun alone, the process with which you carry out tantric sex is also sacred and unique. This process involves rituals and creative techniques that will do a lot of things to you. They will make you feel good, calm your fears, heal your negativity and bad experiences and will even increase your ability to love and have peace.

Tantra sex styles and positions also affect you in many ways. Your body, soul and spirit experience tranquil and your body will experience real growth and changes as you get into the tantra driven ecstatic states with your partner. You will feel the effects of chemicals like endorphins- also known as the pleasure chemical, and oxytocin- cuddle chemical, phenylethylamine and adrenaline from tantric sex practices. The best part about Tantric sex is that you can decide which love chemical you generate by choosing specific tantric practices.

Although no one had ever taken the time to study tantric sex in a laboratory, it is important to note that other related research had proved to us that there are actually some practices that can alter the brain and body to accommodate unusual bliss. Tantric sex happens to incorporate some of these activities in its sexual rituals. For instance, Meditation, which happens to be an important tantric strategy have been found out, through extensive research, to have good effects on the brain wave activity. It helps specifically in generating a relaxation atmosphere.

In a research that was done to prove this statement, a California sexologist measured and compared women's brain wave during relaxation and tantric-related masturbatory activity. The result was that women who practice the tantra masturbatory activity induced their brain waves to get more pleasurable states of consciousness.

TANTRIC SEX AND YOUR ENERGY PATHWAYS

Although it is not commonly known, your body is made up of energy pathways, otherwise known as Chakras. These pathways ensure the conscious flow of energy and drive in your body. With tantric sex, you can be able to discover, control make use of these energy channels and the energy coursing through it. During intense tantric sex, you link those energies with your partner's own to achieve ultimate feelings of unity and cohesion, and ensure an enjoyable sexual activity.

The basics of Tantric sex: "Yes, Yin Yang, Yoni and Yab Yum" that will be discussed later in this eBook incorporate and integrate the vital glands in the brain (the pituitary and pineal glands) with the energy channels or Chakras. The results are always impressive and "out of the world". It is a must try. However, it is important to not get carried away by the awesome bliss that tantric sex offers. The purpose of tantric sex is not solely for individual gain. You shouldn't forget that the main reasons why tantric sex is practiced is to attain enlightenment, wisdom and makes it beneficial to all mankind. That is the ultimate purpose of tantric sex.

CHAPTER THREE: TANTRIC SEX IN AMERICA AND EUROPE

Although Tantric sex started in the practices of the ancient Eastern cultures, it was forgotten and neglected over the years, as a result of the wars, cultural changes and upheavals that characterized the Eastern societies. However, the art of tantric sex is being reviewed, awaken and studied deeply by notable personalities in the field. This is enabled as a result of cultural transfer and exchange. This is when key figures notice some precious ways things are being done in a county and decide to integrate the knowledge of these ways in their home country. Tantric sex was gotten from the Orient, but is being reawakened in the west.

This is not to say that we do not have several notable Easterners, popular in the art of tantric sex practices. Eastern gurus like Sachi dananda and Swamis Muktananda had made meditation- a popular tantric sex practice- to be very popular from as far back as 30 years ago. Another notable personality that links the Eastern and Western thoughts is the Indian mystic Osho. He was popular for adapting Eastern meditation practices effortlessly into the daily activities of Westerners.

Mantak Chia is also evident in making the practices of tantric sex go mainstream. However, in the west, tantric sex practices were awakened by the activities of the students involved in Meditation and Yoga (tantric sex related practice). These students came about the knowledge and teachings of tantra and thereby integrated and joined to their own practices.

Although it has been established that Tantric sex originated from the orient, it is essential to note that the practices are wisely acceptable and appealing to more westerners today. There are several reasons why tantric sex is appealing to the western world. These reasons will be looked into below.

Firstly, Tantric sex steps are simple and easy to carry out. Furthermore, they give fast results which particularly appeal to westerners who are in love with fast lifestyles and quick solutions to problems.

Secondly Tantric sex practices involve the usage and acceptance of desire. Most Americans fancy engaging in ideas that makes them use and channel their desire into something positive and appealing. Since these ideas are rare, they naturally took a liking to Tantric sex.

Unlike several related practices, Tantric sex do not require isolation or joining a cult before you can get involved in its practices. You do not have to step away from the society, recite funny chants, wear robes and even give up your possessions. Westerners do not fancy ideas like that. Tantric sex promises greater results without doing these things, and even aids better communication.

Tantric sex generally works with the principle of energy transformation and stages of energy change. This principle is very familiar to westerners because it is considerably talked about in subjects like physics, technology and electronics.

We all like to be in control and westerners are not exempted. One of the main reasons why tantric sex is popular with westerners is because it allows them to control things, control themselves and also control others. The practices in Tantric sex helps to harness control and carry energy into all the body parts to achieve different purposes.

Perhaps one of the most important reasons why Tantric sex is highly preferred by westerners is because it encourages personal development. The practices help you to be self-determined and gives you daily practical ways to achieve ultimate bliss and peace.

Although Tantric sex firstly involves individual participation, it is very beneficial to the society as a whole. The reason being that, Tantric sex practices aids better communication and relationship with your partner. If you and your partner are happy and at peace, you radiate positive vibes around you and to people that come in contact with you every day. That will help build a good and loving society.

In addition, popular themes in America's motivational topics include personal improvement, self-mastery and self-discovery. Those are the exact watchwords that Tantric sex helps you to achieve.

Another reason why tantric sex is appreciated in the Western world is because its practices helps uphold and explore the beauty of your body. The practices reveal uncommon ways in which you can use and drive your body for peace.

Lastly Tantric sex practices make use of your environment and things you can easily get to help improve your sex life and heighten your senses. These things include, your nice surroundings, attractive clothing, and sweet-smelling perfume

GENERAL MISCONCEPTIONS ABOUT TANTRA AND TANTRIC SEX

Due to Tantra's nature of celebrating and upholding sexuality, tantric sex has been a subject of controversy and criticisms. However, these criticisms arose from little or no understanding about Tantric sex. They are formed based on the general misconceptions and myths about the practice. These myths will be discussed below and would be corrected as well.

Misconception: You sacrifice pleasure when engaging in Tantric sex

Fact: No, you don't. You are not comprising on pleasure and passion when you practice tantric sex. As a matter of fact, your joy and pleasure is heightened when you observe

Tantric sex practices. Tantra is not against sexual pleasure, neither does it consider it immoral or impure. Rather, tantra believes that sex is important in our lives and uses it to achieve states of heavenly bliss, which is even better than earthly pleasure.

Misconception: Tantra is a dangerous religion or cult that brainwash individuals.

Fact: Tantra is neither a cult nor a religion. Tantra do not have the features or characteristics that would qualify it to be an association or a sect. Also, the values and ideals advocated by tantric sex do not aim to control you. Rather, it teaches you how to effectively use and control your sexual desires. From the start to the finish of each tantric sex practice, you are in charge. You make the decisions and choose which tantra practice you want to carry out.

Misconception: Tantric sex allows for satisfying immoral appetites and unchecked sex activities

Fact: Tantric sex do not preach or indulge uncontrolled sexual appetites. In fact, it is against using the practices to satisfy your personal sexual desire. It however helps you be the master of your desires and emotions and assist you in channeling it for higher purposes. Tantra takes sex and connection between two partners seriously, and to practice true tantra, you must be committed to your partner. It is true that some people would have pursued their sexual appetites and have sex with several people in the name of practicing tantra, but this is not what true tantra teaches.

Tantra consider sexuality to be divine and should therefore be held in high respect. Its purpose should not be limited to wanton physical desires. Rather, it should be used by partners to reach a higher state of bliss.

Misconception: Tantric sex turns you into a sex addict

Fact: It is indeed true that tantric sex helps reveal your sexual energy and exposes you to the hidden energy you don't know you have. However, it teaches you how to control this energy. Although Tantric sex gives you room to express yourself, it also teaches you how to overcome and control your sexual feelings. If you learnt Tantric sex well, controlling your sexual tendencies should therefore not be a problem. You should be responsible with the use, because true tantra do not encourage random or unnecessary sex.

Misconception: Tantric sex is mainly for the Eastern world and do not apply to sex realities of Westerners.

Fact: As it has been stated before in this eBook, tantric sex practices are actually agreeable with the sex beliefs of the western world. They both share similar themes and the westerners love it because it gives room for pleasure, and aids individual development.

Misconception: Tantra only deals with sex

Fact: It is important to note that Tantric sex do not deal with sex all the time. In fact there are some practices where you won't even need to touch the genitals of the other partner. Tantric sex is mainly about creating an energetic and spiritual contact or relationship between partners. The use of sexual intercourse or connection of sexual parts only serves the purpose of increasing the energetic and power connection between a couple.

Misconception: Perfecting the art of tantra takes a long time.

Fact: A very important benefit of tantric sex is that the practices are easy to learn and you get to see results immediately you put them into effect. In a week, if you are dedicated, you can learn the vital basic ideas and practices of tantric sex that will help improve your sex life and other aspects of your life.

TEN ESSENTIAL BENEFITS OF PRACTICING TANTRIC SEX

There is no practice that you set your mind to learning, that won't benefit you in the long or short run. There are a lot of perks you get from devoting your time, money and energy to learning Tantric sex practices. Ten of them are hereby listed below.

1.Deepens connection with your partner: Tantric sex opens

your heart more to receive and give love, it shows you how to create and deepen a lasting spiritual and physical connection with your loved one.

2. Improves your health: When you practice Tantric sex, you are improving your overall physical and mental life. Tantric sex practices benefit you physically and psychologically. They restore you from fatigue and also aid your respiratory and breathing system. The essential features of Tantric sex practices which include meditation and relaxation have been proven by researchers to increase good physical, mental and emotional health.

3. Makes you look and feel young: Another essential importance of Tantric sex is it takes care of stresses and gives you health benefits that are essential in making you look and feel young.

.

4. Empower women: Usually women are the weaker partners when it comes to issues involving sex. Some women give in to sex when they are not interested but gave in due to

pressure from their partners. However true Tantric sex practice respects and honours women. You achieve a position of unity and equality with your partner in Tantric sex

5. Empower men: Men face issues and have worries when it comes to their sex life as well. Most times, their worries are always focused around their penis size and the number of minutes/hours they could last in sex. So many men do not also know the proper ways to please a woman during sex. Tantric sex is affording men the chance to feel empowered in sex. Irrespective of your specifications, you will be confident enough and make your partner happy.

6. Attain satisfaction from sex: The reason why sex has become boring and unsatisfactory for you is because you haven't truly connected with your partner. When your sexual act only involves your genitals and leaves the other parts of your body, like your heart, you tend to feel unsatisfied after every sex. With Tantric sex however, you and your partner can achieve a true satisfaction through the energy tantra channels to all the parts of your body.

7 Relieve you from social ills like depression and anxiety: A lot of people suffer from depression and anxieties caused by the society. These social ills can weigh an individual down and in stringent cases, may even lead to death. By performing tantric sex practice however, you get enough energy channeled to your body that helps your mind overcome these worries.

8 Upgrade sex: Tantric sex basically elevates sex from just a physical connection to a spiritual affair which makes it more blissful and impactful.

9. Make lasting pleasure: Tantric sex practices increases the length of your lovemaking as well as the ecstatic feelings you get while having it. Tantric sex techniques help you direct your sexual energy to different parts of the body, giving you a blissful feeling even after ejaculation.

10. Heal wounds gotten from past relationships: With tantric sex, you will be able to effectively let go of your past

emotional breakdowns and disappointments. It heals you and makes you feel loved and wanted.

PART 2

THE BASICS OF TANTRIC SEX: YES, YIN YANG, YONI, AND YAB YUM

As you progress in the learning and study of Tantric sex, you will find your views about life, relationships and the world changing gradually. This new trend in your thought at first might not be comfortable with you, but will surely help your everyday life. You will start seeing men and women beyond their physical image, but as beings that could reach a divine state of higher consciousness. Sex will be elevated from just a physical activity and will assume a spiritual and sacred role. As you learn more, you will learn new languages and positions of love and how you can be able to please your partner more. You will learn about how you and your partner can be deeply connected and achieve a higher level of bliss and consciousness.

However, to make the learning of tantric sex more effective, you have to put on hold any contrasting beliefs or deductions you have, based on the image you want to create or the role your partner has to play in sex. Be ready to accept and adapt to new beliefs and ideas about your individual self, how to achieve more connection with your partner and how to have great sex.

The basic concepts and practices of tantric sex that are essential to your learning will be discussed in detail.

CHAPTER FOUR: YIN AND YANG: MALE AND FEMALE IN TANTRA

A common stereotype that has been believed over the years is the socially engineered difference between men and women. Men are seen as strong and dominating while women are seen as soft and weak. Men are also highly criticized about not expressing their feelings, women as well are said to be less confident and afraid of speaking up. However, in recent times, the gap between the social requirements of men and women have considerably reduced.

One of the main principles of Tantric sex is that male and female are seen as polar opposites with different characteristics. According to the Eastern theory, from which tantric sex originated from, Yang stands for masculine traits while Yin represents feminine features. It doesn't mean however that a male can't be "yin" and a female "Yang"

The purpose of this concept is not to take it literally, rather

32

the two opposite entities should be imagined as separate forces or energies. When these two great forces together, tantra assures that they will create an ultimate bliss.

BALANCING POLARITIES AND UNITING TWO OPPOSITES

The ultimate aim of tantric sex is to create a deep connection and unite two opposites - in this case, the man and the woman. The activity of uniting two opposite sexes is called different names in different traditions. However, all cultures strive to create a link and balance of opposites to attain a high level of consciousness between the two separate energies.

YAB YUM; HOW TO PRACTICE IT

Another vital concept in Tantric sex is yab yum. Yab Yum is a Hindu word that refers to an important position in tantric art. The man sits down and crosses his legs while the woman straddles in his lap. The legs of the man are wrapped around the legs of female and thereby connects behind the back.

Yab yum as a position in tantric sex signifies the unity of action between the opposite sexes. It also represents the union of the separate male and female energies of yin and yang.

Yab Yum is essential because it helps lovers achieve these things namely:

- Allows them to look into each other's eyes, thereby building trust and unity

- Enables lovers to have access to each other's bodies

- Ordinates and connects lover's energy centers

YONI AND LINGAM

Tantra sex doesn't only give you new beliefs about sex. It also updates your vocabularies with new words to call your genitals. The words are specifically used to honour and respect the roles your genitals play in sex and their sacredness.

Yoni in Sanskrit means womb and source, however in tantric sex traditions, it is used to refer to the female's vagina- a woman's sacred temple.

Lingam, vajra, or thunderbolt refers to the male penis. It honours the sacredness of the male phallus and summon the male power of Shiva- the Hindu Lord. Tantric sex does not limit you to these names however, you can call your partner's genitals the common names like penis, pussy, vagina etc. You can even form your own names as long as it makes you feel good about yourself and your partner's body

"YES" OR "NO"

Tantric sex believes that each partner is in control when it comes to engaging in sexual activities and each partner has the will of consent or not. Tantric sex teaches that you are in charge of your body and due permission must be asked by your lover before he/she can reach your sacred space. You are empowered to set your boundaries and given the right to say yes/no to your partner's sexual advances. In tantric sex, you can speak out against disrespect, sexual pressures and uncomfortable touches. When you do this, your lover is able to get in full clear terms what you want and how to please you well. Not only will this improve your self-esteem and confidence in the relationship, it will also help you and your partner achieve a higher spiritual connection.

YOUR BODY IS YOUR TEMPLE AND YOU MUST TAKE CARE OF IT

Tantra sees your body as your temple and a vehicle to reach higher bliss and enlightenment, therefore you must take proper care of it. Tantric sex has no specific fitness routine, but several tantric practitioners couple their sexual activities with some form of yoga. Some Yoga postures originated from tantric love making positions and can make your body fit for Tantric sex. However, you can decide to carry out any fitness routine of your choice. The main goal is keeping your body in a perfect condition to effectively carry out tantric sex practices.

CHAPTER FIVE: THE IMPORTANCE OF YOUR BREATH

In Tantra art, your breath is very vital to the success and outcome of a tantric sex practice. When you breathe properly, the necessary oxygen your cells require to function well will be supplied. A proper breathing helps you free your emotions and sensuality. The breath is a main factor affecting the life and length of your sex. Euphoria, organisms, deep intimacy are all hinged on how you control your breath while having sex.

Controlling your breath sounds simple, but in reality, it isn't. This is due to the fact that we hold our breath too much and engage more in shallow breathing. This is not healthy and bad for our sex life. There are three vital practices that you can do to improve your breathing and your sexual energy. The first practice is called the Source of Life. To do this, identify the place where your breath is coming, in your body. It may be from your chest, stomach area or throat. After locating it, ensure that the breath is firmly rooted within your body. Locate the breath and make it come as low down as your sexual organs.

You have to be sitting to carry out the second practice known as "Egg to Eagle". On a sitting position, breath out as you try to form a ball, with your elbows close to your body and hands places on the back of your head. Breathe in, while rising gradually and placing your elbows as far back as you can. Can you feel the stretch in your body now? Push your chest out and arch your back. You will feel air rushing into your lungs. Repeat till your breathing is normal.

The last exercise helps you take in as much air as you can get. It is called the bellows, because you are going to imagine your lungs are a bellows as air rush into them. To start it, make sure your arms are by your side then blow out all your hair in a forceful way. Then, take in as much air as possible. Blowing out and taking in air will come with a lot of noise, but don't be afraid, it is part of the process. Do this repetitively and you will find your breath getting better.

In conclusion it is advisable to engage in breathing practices then and now because they are cogent in helping you direct sexual energy to other parts of the body. Good breath during sex will give perks such as deep connection with the partner, achievement of high bliss and ecstasy and overall maintenance of health.

TANTRIC SEX AND THE CHAKRA WHEELS

Everything in our world today is controlled by energy. Human beings also have energy within them. The feeling you have when you are attracted to a person, or you feel an electricity like jolt when you are around the person you love is caused by energy within you.

Tantric philosophy holds that the energy centers in a human body known as Chakras pass an imaginary axis, from the bottom of our pelvis to top of our head, down to the core of our physical body. Although physical body parts are illustrated but these energy fields aren't physical, rather they are associated with different features. The energy forces spin in a wheellike motion from the seven different centers in your body. The seven chakras throughout the body are associated with colors, sounds, and issues.

It is important to know and understand the workings of the

chakras, because they are integral to tantric sex practices. With Tantric sex practices however, you will be able to attain your desired sex goals and establish that deep connection with your partner.

Perhaps of all the seven, the second chakra can be said to be the most vital, because it is located in your genitals area. It controls the force and energy distributed to the other centers of the body. As a matter of fact, most of the tantric sex practices are best learnt and carried out using the energy from the second chakra.

BREATHING WITHIN THE CHAKRAS

As it has been stated earlier in this eBook, your breathing is very important to tantric sex. Proper breathing assists you by creating a channel in your body through which air can get to your chakras. The air will work with your chakras to energize you, cleanse and heal you.

When air passes through a clear channel in your body, it will make a flutelike sound. This sound signifies that the air is properly coursing through the channels and going past your chakras. When you exhale, you can send your breath to your partner. After feeling it, and going through his/her chakras, he/she can return it to you and you will both be empowered. There are two popular exercises that helps your air flow properly through the chakras. They have been explained in detail   below.

- The first exercise is known as the complete breath. Its purpose is mainly for relaxation. To do this, breathe in deeply into your lower belly or chest. This will make your belly pop out, giving your belly an extra fat look, but it is only temporary. This practice can be carried out alone or with your partner. It is however a good breath practice to do in the middle of a sex. It helps create a deep connection and mutual ease.

- The second breath exercise, is meant to increase your energy and excite you. Commonly known as "fire breath", it works by you inhaling and breathing out of the nose rapidly. This will make your stomach produce a regular throbbing sensation or sound in line with the rapid breaths. Raising and lowering your arms will help increase the energy level of this exercise.

It is important to practice breathing exercises with your partner because it can greatly benefit your sexual life and achieve a lasting love connection.

THE THIRD EYE BELIEF IN TANTRA

There is a popular phrase about the eyes being the window to the soul. Tantra ascribes to this phrase, however not your physical eyes. The eye that Tantra considers leading to your soul is not your real eyes but the significant eye called the third eye.

In practical terms, this third eye can be found behind your real eyes, in the middle of your brain. Tantra believes that opening your third eye, will help you observe more, and understand yourself better. Also, there is a higher level of connection and enlightenment with your partner that can only be achieved with the third eye.

To utilize your third eye better, you can practice this third eye exercise. Put your finger on a spot on your forehead to connect with the third eye and imagine yourself breathing into it to get deeper understanding and relaxation. To make it more effective, you might need to close your eyes.

THE INNER SMILE

The benefits of smiling in an individual's life cannot be overemphasized. It is perfect for expressing happiness and bliss. It increases your confidence and makes you look younger and more attractive. Smiling is beneficial to the society, since it makes you and everybody that comes in contact with you happier. According to research, when you smile, you trigger the limbic system in the brain. An important function of the limbic system is to send pleasure signals to the brain. The smile that is being talked about in the above lines is the outward visible smile that everybody sees.

However, tantra also teaches another type of smile known as the inner smile. The inner smile is imagined. You picture of happening in the primitive brain (which is believed to be at the back of your brain, near the nape of your neck).

Imagining this smile will help create a positive feeling and attitude, and will also reach an higher state of bliss which is the goal of tantra. Putting on the outer and inner smile is the key to ultimate happiness. While showing others your pretty smile, imagine yourself smiling beautifully within too. Not only will this boost your self-esteem and confidence, good vibes and energy will radiate from you inside out.

PLAY THE ROLE OF A PARTICIPANT AND OBSERVER

A vital technique to keep your mind in shape for tantra is by putting yourself in a mental state where you are able to play the role of a participant and observer. It means you are actively doing a thing and yet, you are observing yourself while carrying out this activity. Watching yourself act is called being the witness in common terms. This practice is good for every aspects of your life that can get better with tantra especially sex. Sometimes, sex is affected by the distracting thoughts that course through the minds of the man and woman while in the act. The man might be worryig about how long he will last or if he would be able to please the lady. The lady on the hand might be having doubts about the man's genuine feeling for her. These thoughts reduce the chances of having good sex. Fighting these thoughts or trying to conceal them is not the solution. Tantra advocates that you notice or witness yourself having these thoughts (observe) then simply redirect your attention on your breath and sensational feelings in your body.

CHAPTER SIX: THE CONCEPT OF GOD/GODDESS IN TANTRA

Tantra leads you to God- It gives you a heavenly feeling while on Earth through its sacred tantric sex practices. To achieve a deep connection with the spiritual, you and your lover must have been united together in a higher state of enlightenment. Tantra sees every man and woman as a god or a goddess. It means human beings are created with divine god-like characteristics and abilities that can only be unlocked through self-recognition and adulation. When you honor or "sing praises" of yourself or your beloved, you are mainly awakening the god/goddess in them. Recognizing the god in you and your partner helps to improve your self-esteem and confidence.

The significance and importance of the god and goddess in yourself, as well as its role in tantric sex will be discussed below.

WHAT IS "GOD/GODDESS"?

In Layman's terms, god and goddess refer to some divine beings that have showed supernatural abilities in their relation with man. Although tantra believes in the known gods and goddesses too, however it is more focused on affording yourself and your loved one, the care, honour and respect you give to these divine beings.

Tantra recognises the presence of deities in its practice. The deities are seen in form of spirits, angels and guides. In Tantric sex, these deities symbolise different energies and qualities integral to Tantra views. Although these deities are seen as external beings, Tantra believes that they project some common human-like qualities. We have both male and female deities, and they are given different names which include, daka and dakini, priest and priestess and so on. Of all these names however, goddess is used more to identify the female deity in the tantra community. The goddess is seen as a powerful female with several impressive qualities that ranges from soft to fierce. However, the term "god" is not as wisely used because of the high reverence and honour attached to the Judeo-Christian "God" who is believed to be the creator of things.

Tantra believes that being "god" or "goddess" is your birthright and it doesn't have to be another life. The energy, power and divine attributes that course through you is enough reason to be god or goddess. Irrespective of age, culture, status and race, all human share these amazing godlike qualities. Every woman is a goddess because she shares feminine features that are usually ascribed to a goddess - lover, planner, seducer and all other feminine qualities. To fully attain the feeling of a goddess, a woman must believe she has these qualities, and should be honoured by her partner. This goes for men too, who share godlike characteristics. He must also be revered and honoured.

WHY LOVERS SHOULD WORSHIP EACH OTHER

The importance of worshipping your partner and vice versa in your relationship can't be overemphasized. When you complement your partner, it means you acknowledge their activities and presence in your life, and you appreciate them.

In tantric sex, when you are enjoined to worship your partner, you are asked to love him or her unconditionally and timelessly. It doesn't mean making your relationship a master-slave relationship or turning a blind eye to the faults and mistakes of your partner. Rather, the act of worship in tantric sex helps create mutual respect and honour among partners. For a tantric sex practice to be efficient, you must worship your partner like a god or goddess.

PART 3

GETTING STARTED IN TANTRIC SEX

By now we should be breathing at our best and powerfully channeling the right amount of sexual energy from our own body, down to that of our intimate partner. To the extent in which, you are now more control dominant and can determine your own time to speed it up or to simmer down as you lose yourself into beatitude.

Now let's take this a notch higher, here you will be acquiring immense knowledge of designated drills to up the ante and also drills on when to step down your sexual energy at your own will, to prepare you for a lengthy but satisfying lovemaking. You'll find out how to see love through the right perspective and learn skills to key you deeply into sensuality beyond your wildest imagination.

We will walk you through the clandestine of the heart hold, sacrum tap and the definite muscle locks which links the pathway to sexual pleasure. You'll learn to penetrate through any obstacle hindering you from clinging to pure bliss or holding you back from unlocking new levels of elevated stages for love. Getting ready, your mind, your soul and your body as a love edifice.

CHAPTER SEVEN: READY YOUR EDIFICE OF LOVE

In this part, you will get to know and learn:

- How to love your body
- The duo colors of tantra
- The right way to keep the spine straightened and in good health
- The Tantric way of dieting right
- How your Tantric way can be aided by White tantra
- The Inner muscle grips that aid better sex control

Tantric practice suggestively imposes that your body is your edifice and therefore it must be kept healthy and ready for your journey to beatitude. Here, you will be introduced to certain tenets and regular drills that aid you in honoring this edifice.

YOUR BODY AS THE ROUTE TO BEATITUDE

During the course of studying tantra, anticipate an experience of thrill and glee. An impulsive surge of energy will be observed flowing through your spine, exciting every cell in your body from the sole of your feet to the top of your head. Your whole body will now become a route between the terrestrial and the metaphysical enroute beatitude.

Paint a scenario in your head. Picture yourself as an engine. But to understand this better, you will need to retrace your steps to our study on Chakra or the energy core. As in an engine, your gas reservoir is your sex core, the tires and chassis are the first chakra or base core which aids you cling to the road (The first chakra duty is to groom you). Your breath blends with your sexual energy (In similitude with how air mixes with gas in an engine) serving as the ignition through your spine. The muscle grips as will be depicted later are the spark plugs.

Every system in your car which includes: The electrical parts, the exhaust, the battery and the ignition are very much akin to every system in your body (Nervous, Endocrine and Circulatory) all need to be working in tandem for you to move with consummate ease on the highway while performing at maximum operating efficiency.

On few occasions we barely take cognizance of the body edifice we possess and dwell in. At times, it seems we take it for granted until we feel pains, get sick or totally breakdown. Other times when we get to look in the mirror we get irritated and depressed by what we behold, forgetting in most cases we could have prevented it. Worst, we abuse our body edifice with poisonous food, insufficient sleep (I guess we are all in this together because a few times I have been guilty of this!), overfeeding, Alcohol and drugs intake and sometimes even sex we felt we wanted but ended up regretting.

Another way we have abused our body is self-criticism, which most times is based on unhealthy comparison with others and in many ways is not constructive or encouraging. But to prepare yourself for Tantric love, you must be prepared to discard this negative self-criticism for the greater good. You must be ready to channel all your energy from body hate to body love.

DEVELOPING BODY LOVE

The basis of every sex therapeutical seminar over the past two decades have all circled around appreciating your body. And overtime you have to learn to imbibe the lessons you will be learning here till it becomes a part of you. This involves you gazing at your body and deliberately modifying any undesirable attitude. Drills which end up enhancing your pleasure should be seen as fun while carrying them out rather than work. Work doesn't increase pleasure rather it subdues pleasure and, in its place, introduces stress. These exercises recommended below should be carried out on your private parts and body in entirety:

1. **Stand stark nude in front of a complete (not shortened) mirror.** It is recommended you do this immediately after your bath. Gaze at every part of your body beginning from the sole of your feet, gradually moving up, to the top of your head. If you get caught in a moment and you find yourself criticizing, without hesitation, halt and utter soothing words instead. For instance, rather than say "My boobs are too small for my age" it becomes "my boobs are relatively nice and firm, perfect for my age" or "my thighs

are too massive" becomes "my thighs are beautiful and strong ". I have come across a few ladies with low self-esteem because of the size and shape of their backside. I heard them say words like "My butt is totally out of sorts" you should rather say words like "My butt is well rounded and moderate". Say these encouraging words and feel the magic.

Don't get unhealthy fixation that you are not telling the truth. Never feel like you are lying to yourself. What you are simply doing is just redirecting your focus and being less harsh on yourself by saying those gentle words.

2. **Observe your genitals.** The feminine genitals is less conspicuous than that of the men. So, a lady is very much likely to need to be in a sitting position on a bed while utilizing a hand mirror and flashlight to aid her see better. Open your inner vagina lips and look out for its shape, moisture and color.

3. **Observe your first chakra** (Your symbol of security, your base core is located around your anal area). For both

male and female, the easiest position to take while doing this is by Squatting. Just as in the genital observation for ladies, Men can also utilize a hand mirror and flashlight to see more lucidly. Look out for skin texture and colors.

DEPICT YOUR SEXUAL PART THOROUGHLY

Gazing at the genitals comes off so easily for most men, because their genitals are so noticeable and accessible anytime they step into the bathroom. But it is the exact opposite for women, as they have been taught not to look. Even in this present time and age, most females are extremely shy or very uncertain of what lies underneath. Most times, sexuality activists are stunned and left in awe at how little even the most enlightened men and women know about their sexual parts. Growing up, most people know little to nothing about their sexual part. Their mother or father basically just gave them books to read and left them to sort it out on their own. This only aided my confusion, until they were probably into their early 20's before they could understand that which was written in those books. Below some comparing descriptions of your body to certain figures will be made, which portray the important parts of the male and female genitalia.

The following should be noted by both sexes (Male and Female):

1.) Around the pelvic region, lies actual sets of muscles which includes those around the opening leading to the anus, and those around the genitals. They are essentially involved in excitement and sexual toning. They are termed as the Love Muscles, you will get to know about them as we go a lot deeper in this chapter.

2.) The Sacrum is a triangular like area just above the tailbone which when tapped triggers energy, as will further be explained later on as you keep reading.

3.) The Kundalini gland is the site of energy for beatitude that lies inactive within the spine awaiting activation by the triggers of Tantric practices. It so often is portrayed artistically like a coiled snake.

An attentive look at the anatomy of the female gender show;

1.) The Clitoris is so much more than the tip that you most times feel. In reality, it possesses a lengthy shaft that extends into the body, which is pleasurable to stimulate to a certain degree.

2.) The opening of the Urethral is not in front of the vaginal opening, rather it is separated from the vaginal opening. It is a singular opening though it functions in tandem with the vaginal opening.

3.) Surrounding the Urethra lies a sponge-like tissue (called the "urethral sponge", comprising the ducts, glands and blood vessels) which secretes fluids emitted via the urethra during an elated state of arousal. Female ejaculate also referred to as "Love Juices" can be activated from the inner stimulation within the vagina in the feminine space (popularly known as G-spot).

An attentive look at the masculine anatomy portrays that you can reach (and arouse) the prostate gland from the external along the perineum and from the internal via the opening leading to the anus as will be depicted in subsequent chapters.

JUST IMAGINE IF YOUR SEXUAL PARTS COULD SPEAK

But just imagine if your penis could talk? What would it say? Or if your vagina could utter words? What words would it utter? Funny imagination I guess, personally I laughed out loud at the thought of it. But in reality, the truth is, at specific times our bodies have spoken and in one way or the other, we have responded. Now imagine your body asking you questions such as "Why do you question my size? " or "Why can't I just have a break? " or "Why can't I be adored"? or "Why can't you cherish me"? Or "Why can't I be treated as the edifice I am? ". How you respond is totally up to you.

CARRY OUT A PHYSICAL EXAMINATION OF YOUR GENITAL

Take sessions of deep breathing, centralize yourself. Now you should gaze at your genitals, touch them with the main intent of physical examining. Look out for the colors, textures and shapes. After carrying this physical examination with the bigger picture ahead, get emotionally entangled. Let yourself freely touch your genitals with pleasure stationed in mind. Observe what you can as you look in the mirror or presumably lie back and just get totally immersed in the sensation. Concentrate on the smallest of sensations, without any heightened expectations.

CHAPTER EIGHT: THE DUO COLORS OF TANTRA: THE PHYSICAL AND SEXUAL BONDING

There are basically two types of drills or colors of tantra. You will get to know so much more about them as you keep reading this book. They are:

1.) *White Tantra* which refers to the drills which involves more of the physical and are related to yoga and other form of Physical fitness.

2.) *Red tantra* refers to the drills that are in its entirety sexual in nature or utilize immense sexual energy, channeled in a highly metaphysical manner.

The Yoga Bond

Yoga is easily the most famous of the general white tantra paths. So many Tantric masters also double as Yoga masters who have learned and practiced the different poses for a large chunk of years. Yoga aids you drive your focus on your body, calm your mind, strengthen and stretch your body and also direct your movements. All this can aid you achieve ejaculatory domination and orgasms in multiples, and profit your entire health as well as the terrestrial experience of the super eminent energy you share with whom you love.

Take a programme at a local yoga center or contact any workshops or check out for any Websites that aids in location of any Tantra Community to know if they offer yoga tutorials. Like most tantra workshops, they will introduce you to simple yoga drills.

SOME SIMPLE MOTION IN YOGA

Here you would be given a brief depiction of a few simple motions in Yoga portrayed in many individual based routines. You will get to learn interesting yoga poses you can easily carry out with your lover as you keep reading:

1.) **The Head Lift:** Stand erect, as straight as possible. Stretch your head up to the sky like a string were pulling it upwards from the centre of your crown. Breathe in through your nose, pulling your shoulder blades back toward each other. Breathe out and press your feet firmly into the ground, as if you getting yourself rooted like a tree. Relax and redo continually.

2.) **The Cobra Pose:** Extensively lie fully on the floor on your stomach. Place your hands direct under your shoulders, arms close to your body with elbows held back, and in slow motion lift the upper body and head in a curve, looking upward.

3.) **The Cat Pose**: After carrying out the cobra pose, bring your head down slowly and lift the knees up, then position make your back round, to the extent in which the spine can be stretched in the opposite direction to the cobra pose.

4.) **The Resting Pose**: Now the first three poses have been carried out, here comes the resting pose. After ensuring you carried out every step of the cat pose to the very last detail, lower your chest to your knee level and place your forehead to the ground while your arms are outstretched. Breathe with ease as it comes naturally to you.

THE BANDHAS

As observed overtime tantra breathing drills and yoga postures require your body parts are held in specific ways or brings out noticeable muscular contractions to dictate your energy. These drills are referred to as the *Bandhas*. They are very similar in action to the waterway locks, as energy is put together in a specific area by bringing about firming of muscles there, the energy then is allowed to escape in a stronger force in directions of your choice (throughout the spine or wherever it is directed to).

The 3 most utilized holds are:

- **The Throat hold**: To carry this out, breathe in and tilt your chin downwards to your throat while making the back of your neck straight, lift your chin and breathe out slowly.

- **The Belly Hold**: Breathe out, tuck in your navel backwards in the direction of your spine, and move your stomach up toward your throat.

- **The Pelvis Hold:** Make firm your pubococcygeal and

anal sphincter muscles (more discussion on how to exercise the pubococcygeal muscles will be done in the next section)

The bandhas is of immense gain to your sexual life. This is why:

The three-step lock combines all three of the common holds and aids men to be in full control of their ejaculation without losing their erection. Breathe in and practice the throat hold. Breathe out and carry out the belly hold. Press on the pubococcygeal muscles for the pelvis hold. Redo.

- *Pelvis holds* aids both sexes (male and female) to fortify the muscles around the pelvic region. This action leads to more powerful orgasms.

- *Muscle holds* aid both sexes in the conditioning of their body in entirety, fortifies the lower back muscles and amplifies the outcome of love muscle activity which lead to an elevated level of sensation during of pleasuring of self or intimate sexual bonding with your partner. The greatest advantage of these holds, is that it can be done anytime and anywhere.

Before carrying out yoga drills, ensure you:

- Regularly check in with a doctor before you kick off any yoga program.

- At least warm up for a few minutes before starting your routine.

- Don't push your body beyond its handling capacity.

- Take time out to rest your body when you feel any tiredness.

- Maintain your balance during those routines (If you tilt to the left during a bend, ensure you tilt to your right too)

LOVE MUSCLE ACTIVITIES FOR BOTH SEXES

For women, their pubococcygeal muscles runs from the sides of the entrance to the vagina. Fortifying and toning these muscles lead to more moments of pleasure during sex for the women and also for her partner. It also aids in tightening the muscles, mostly after childbirth). Locate these muscles and press on them, very similar to when trying to hold back urine, and then let go as if pushing urine out. Now intentionally narrow them in increased tempo progression for around 30 seconds. Daily put this into action at various times.

For the men, the pubococcygeal muscles routes through the perineum and links to both the scrotum and anus. In similitude, to the steps for the women locate the pubococcygeal muscles and press on them, as if trying to prevent the flow of urine. Make it narrow and let go 10 times, at an increasing tempo, various times daily. This is a very effective drill to aid men be in full control of their timing of ejaculation.

Narrowing and letting go of the anal sphincter muscles for both men and women also leads to elevated sexual pleasure. Find out the location of these muscles by pressing on, as if to stop defecation, then bear down as if pushing yourself to nullify.

ADHERE TO AN AWARE WORKOUT

Various workouts exist that will definitely tone your body and fortify you. They serve as complements to your sexual tantric drills as long as you keep alert as you put them into practice. This implies you redirect your focus on how that specific activity is channeling your energy and how your breathing is in motion. These workouts may include:

- *Western style workouts* like Aerobics, weightlifting or designated routines from your personal trainer.

- *Eastern style drills* like the popular Tai chi or the more popular Qipong are different systems of Yoga movements in China which opens up the body to allow flow of life-forcing energy. The T'ai chi Bo balancing aids build a firm and flexible back. The Bagua Xun Dao Gong is known for stretching and strengthening the legs.

THE SPINAL TAP

Being in possession of a healthy spine is very essential to the drills of Tantric sexuality. The spine is the route of breath through the body, from the first chakra(base) all through to the top of the head (the crown) . It transfers sexual energy from the genitals through the body and straight into the head for awakening and transformation.

Give great attention to your spine and how it is positioned at any point in time. How it is when you sit? How it is when you stand? How it is when you walk? Your spine is responsible for whatever posture you take. So, it is essential we take the right postures for a healthy spine.

As we grow old everyone gets really bothered about looking slumped over in posture. Aesthetically, it isn't a beautiful sight to behold but also it disrupts breathing patterns and affects the breath carrying life energy through your body termed *Pana*. Give special attention and treatment to your spine, it is really precious. See a doctor if need be for proper spine alignment and positioning.

YOU ARE THE OUTCOME OF WHAT YOUR FOOD INTAKE

A saying goes thus *"You are what you eat"*. Whatever you take in as food is what you eventually become. Food is a fuel to the body and an energy generator. It has been researched fatty foods are detrimental to your general health and also eating heavy meals is not encouraging for good sex. Though, healthy eating habits go beyond those facts, they must be imbibed in your whole Tantric life routine.

An obstructed or impure digestive tract can lead to disruption in flow of energy. Several tantric practicing individuals occasionally carry out "Cleansing" to purify their systems of toxins. Cleansing ranges from eating just raw foods down to drinking juice. Everyone has different body shapes and sizes, so all approaches don't work for every individual with the same effects. Ensure you find which approach works for you, get medical advice or read books that enlighten you on nutrition the tantric way or get recommendations from experienced tantra pedagogues.

Note:

Never forget your body is an edifice of love, so carry out your exercise routines with your body as motivation. It promotes health and enhances your sexual energy while preparing you for tantric sex. Take care of your spine and stick to a healthy eating plan.

CHAPTER NINE: SPEED UP OR SUPPRESS YOUR ENERGY LEVEL

In this chapter you will know and learn:

- No one else is in charge of your energy besides you
- Drills to simmer down your energy
- To utilize air yoga for stress reduction
- Drills to speed up your energy
- Chakra thump, sacrum tap and pelvic thrusts to shake up your shakti energy
- How your partner can also be your assistant

Now your body is presently in a good shape, you can easily move to the next phase which is being in control of your energy by relaxing or speeding it up as part of your tantric practice. It's essential we get enlightened on these two states due to their consistency with the tantric principles of opposites. This implies, energy can be calm or vibrant, fluid or in motion. You need to acquire knowledge on how to channel your energy in both directions.

Here you will be enlightened on the right exercises to put you in a relaxed mood, with your sex energy at a cool, fluid pace or to speed you up till you fully energy charged. Keep in mind it's only you who can control your body edifice, as long as you are well prepared it responds to all your triggers for its action.

SIMMER DOWN: METHODS TO APPLY

Life is extremely demanding, so it is quite understandable there will be difficulties in attempting some of the tantric practices when your mind isn't in the right frame. Work burden, health issues or a relationship crisis could hinder you from channeling energy in the way you desire.

Here are some methods to help you calm down while resting your energy:

- **Take charge of your breathing:** Inhale deeply in the count of seven and breathe out on a lengthier count (as is within your capacity). Breathing out much longer than you breathe in tends to relax you and enhances heart rate reduction.

- **Sit in a fixed position and pour out your mind**. Allow your thoughts enter and exit without shifting focus to a specific one or meditate on a word to soothe your mind.

- **Modify your surroundings** to kick out distractions in form of ringing phones or disrupting street noise.

- **Soak yourself** in a cozy bubble bath amidst lit candles.

- **Go on long walks** or toss a ball around with little kids. Any form of physical activity is an exemplary *Stress Reducer*. Just ensure you do it.

- **Eyes closed, picture a calming scene**. A beautiful scenery as the ocean fulfills this purpose. Just imagine the beach sands in between your toes. Simply picture a soothing and amazing scene.

- **Massage yourself calmly**. Apply smooth, lengthy strokes to provide you soothe while you breathe deeply at a slow pace. Spread cream over your skin with every hand glide.

AIR YOGA AS A MEANS OF STRESS REDUCTION

You probably already have the foundational ideology of yoga, that's if you don't already put it into practice. But I doubt you know what Air Yoga actually is or its essence. Air Yoga is a captivating deviation to a more traditionally known yoga which implements the tantric principles. Developed by Joshua Smith a tantric teacher and resident of Washington DC. It includes body movement into the more traditional yoga postures, allowing your body settle conveniently into positions it feels need to be in.

Begin by taking one of the simplest yoga pose, the *tree* pose. Stand feet shoulder width apart while bending your knees slightly, eyes gazing down. Breathe out deeply via the mouth, shifting focus to a specific spot on the ground, dropping deeper and deeper into your body each time, breathing out. Eyes closed, breathe in via the nose, lift your head and allow your hands move upwards. While breathing via the mouth, let your arms arch forward, allowing the head and body be led softly to the ground. Relax your hands, arms, jaw and shoulders.

Align yourself as directed by your spine and body, in whichever way it chooses. This is a deviant to any other yoga. Stay tantrically conscious of your breathing pattern and you will be eased into a transcendent calmness.

GOOD LOVING: SPEEDING IT UP

Definitely, at certain times you don't feel up for sex either due to tiredness or lack of interest, even if a little chunk of you drives your urge to have sex or fulfil you partners sexual desire. There's delightful news written here, as there is an abundance of tantric sex practices, which aid in energizing your body to make love.

BE IN CHARGE OF YOUR BREATHING

Inhale deeply in a count of seven and breathe out to a lesser count. Breathing in longer than you breathe out enhances your heart rate. You can also practice the *Fire Breath,* this involves you breathing in and breathing out swiftly via the nose. Allow your stomach get filled up and then deflate with the air.

PUTTING THE SACRUM TAP INTO ACTION

Strike lightly on your sacral area (it lies slightly above your tailbone end and below your waist). This is the residence of immense energy termed the *Kundalini energy* because it is discharged from the kunda glands. Some tantra workshops taught by Tantrika International, often involve more detailed variations of this drill.

PERFORM THE CHAKRA THUMP

Awaken the energy in your Chakra by tapping on any of them. Make swift repetitive upwards and downwards tapping movements on the body with the finger pads. Also make a fist and use the softer sides of your hands.

APPLY STREAMING

Streaming is a deviation of the previous drills. The giver strikes forcefully on either side of the receiver spine with the fingertips, beginning at the sacrum and gradually getting upwards to the neck. You could carry out a massage when you get to the shoulders.

DANCE AS AN ENERGETIC FORCE

The gains from dance as a motion, body conditioner and fun giver are limitless. Put on some good at home and just let go of yourself to its rhythm, sway, tilt and shake. There's enough room for improvisation, so improvise. Imagine yourself being a professional ballet dancer or Chinese god or goddess wielding a sword like a knight in shining armour. Having a partner is not really a necessity. Put into consideration taking a dance class of any kind.

PUT YOUR PELVIS IN MOTION

The Pelvic thrust is important to producing the right amount of sexual energy and pleasure in sex. Carrying them out is a boost for your sexual energy. This is the motion men naturally make when having sex but mostly don't extend for long to achieve its genuine benefits.

Pelvic thrusts are one of the highly favored and fun drills in any tantra workshop. It makes for an awe-inspiring sight beholding a room filled with both men and women standing or lying on the floor, backs arched and pelvis thrust forward. Adding sound to the motion is a sweetener.

Pelvic thrust can easily be done from a standing position, moving gradually in progression to the floor via different squatting levels or it could be done in the reverse (from lying down to a raising up). Carrying them out basically involves thrusting the pelvis forward and backward. It's essential to have our breath in order (Breathe out through the mouth as you thrust forward and breathe in through the nose while arching backwards). Once we can carry this out with ease, you move your arms alongside to help your energy motion. While doing this drill alone, you can easily picture yourself thrusting against your partner, having sex to aid you get all sexy and really seductive.

GET YOUR FANTASY GAME ON

It's a healthy norm painting sexual fantasies of probably previous events or arousing imaginary situations. Permit yourself to have these thoughts freely with no holding back on its being good or bad. However, don't get too distracted as tantric drills requires of you that attention is driven towards your body sensations and your present so you can be fully grateful for the real experience, your intimate partner and momentary happenings.

FREE YOURSELF

A popular track has in its lyrics "Let It Go", but in this scenario you have to let yourself go. One of sexual energy buildup rules is releasing your thoughts and motion from any stopping blocks. One way to achieve this is *The Dynamic Meditation,* developed by Osho an Indian mystic.

The *Dynamic Meditation* is done in various sections. The first involves the body shaking for 15mins, inhaling and exhaling swiftly and forcefully. After which you flap your arms, just to get energy flowing. Set your mind free and loosen your jaws while setting your limbs flying. Energy bolts will increase via your body and every cell will tingle with life. Stop suddenly and dive into silence as you meditate to swallow up energy. After carrying this out, free yourself to dancing activities and unhindered fun.

CARRYING OUT THE "SHAKTI SHAKE"

A different way you can trigger your energy is by carrying out the "Shakti Shake". This is an awesome skill to learn. It is very plain and easy to do, get some music playing in the background you know gets you in the groove. Begin with the right leg shaking, then to the left leg. Keep up with the music beat and tempo. Sway your hips while keeping your arms and hands in motion. Shoulders rocking, free your head. Now the whole body is in motion. Observe how lively you feel.

ESSENCE OF LAMA BREATHS

One of the most reliable ways to speed up is the *Lama Breathing*. It is tested and trusted as it has been found out that it is effective in warming the body. Here are two of the basic skills adapted by groups with immense results:

- Stand in an upright position, knees slightly bent and shoulder-width apart. Breathe in and lift your arms outstretched sideways. Breathe out, dropping your arms sideways, blow air out and make bellow like sound till your arms are resting at your sides. Observe your feeling. Redo 3 times.

- Stand rooted firmly to the ground, legs shoulder-width apart. Breathe in and lift one arm, form a fist high above your head and only drop it when breathing out, blowing out air with force while letting a sound out. Regularly change arms (Twice is good enough).

Your Partner As Your Assistant

All drills so far in this chapter can be performed solely (without needed assistance from anyone) or with a partner. Allowing your partner know your sexual energy levels and your willingness to align to his/her keen interest, goes a long way in enhancing trust and intimacy between you.

An establishment of understanding between couples is essential when it comes to sexual energy. For instance, after a bad day in the office Cynthia felt drained and depressed, John her partner had pictured a beautiful evening with her, but after noticing her countenance. He questioned her and she opened up, this made it easier for her to relax and meditate as John understood and ensured he helped her through the process.

Note:

Channeling energy solely or with a partner prepares you for sharing memorable nights of pleasure together. Be in charge of your energy and determine the right moments to be sexual. You can calm or speed up your energy via different breathing patterns and certain drills and be open with your energy levels so you don't disappoint your partner.

CHAPTER TEN: PREPARING THE PLATFORM FOR TANTRIC PLEASURE NIGHTS

- In this chapter you will to know and learn:
- To set aside time for lovemaking
- To prepare for your tantric pleasure nights
- The bathing rites
- The desiring igniting god and goddess attires
- To put the edifice of love and love altar
- The right things to do and right places to go on your tantra date

Imagine lovemaking as your Tantric Date, a unique get together set into 2 steps: *The Plan* and *The Preparation* to experience your night of pleasure and spending time together. Having sex isn't just an act. It is a rite experience that demands thoughts and deliberate actions as a fraction of seduction.

Every action fulfils various purposes which includes Quietening the mind, setting you into the right mood, building anticipation and honoring your partner. Dress yourself and also the intended space for lovemaking, give meticulous attention to the tiniest bit of details. Attention to details is a sign you honor each other and your time together, it shows the value placed on each other and your intimate relationship. Your tantric night of pleasure only begins when you set time aside to be together. Some partners neglect this part.

CRAFTING OUT THE RIGHT AMOUNT OF TIME FOR LOVE

A common complaint from couples is the lack of time for sex. They always feel there's never enough time for

sex. Time for sex is totally dependent on both partners availability, you should be able to create enough time and so should your partner. Really, what could be more important than creating time for this sort of loving, instead it is replaced by work or other activities.

Create time for each other to carry out these drills. Begin

with an hour on 2 separate occasions during the week. Agree on specific time and note time on your calendar. This will serve as a verification of the primary importance of your relationship to you.

However, every new drill or of self-improvement effort requires spending time and dedicating effort to make it a success, be it weightlifting or yoga. To aid you place your priorities right in this world of energy draining, time demanding activities, you deliberately have to schedule yourself in order not to get carried away at first, then later you can be more random. A calendar and a schedule plan go a long way in helping you create time for whom you love.

THE DELIBERATE TIDYING UP

You probably remember the experience of you dressing absolutely stunning as to the best of your ability or carrying out a swift tidying up just in case you have to bring your date back to your place (Throwing clothes in the closet. Sweeping the necessary places meticulously and to great extremities). If you've been together for a lengthy period and don't cherish each other presence, it's simply a hint you need to throwback to those days of dating when you made conscious efforts to genuinely impress. Put into consideration these 10 tips for deliberate tidying up, both alone or with your partner and feel the magic:

- Always ensure your fingernails clean and neatly cut. Neatly trimmed clean nails are attractive (Dirty nails are turnoffs for both sexes) and essential for maintaining a good hygiene because your fingers sometimes serve as simulators on your partner skin or to pleasure her organs.

- Brush your teeth daily, particularly before a romantic time with your partner. Like nails an unbrushed teeth are the toppers on the list of turnoffs for men and women. Utilize a baking soda inclusive toothpaste for really good cleansing and a nice mouthwash for that extra bit of freshness.

- Wash each other's hair. Particularly when a man does it to his woman, as it is a rarely seen action.

- Shave her, paying special attention to being soft on her skin. Putting trust in him to carry this out will make him feel proud and pleased. The woman should also do same for her man.

- Do his nails. Paint her toenails too.

- Modify the bathroom lighting. Most bathrooms have harsh lighting. Replace the bulbs with really nice colored ones for special evenings that creates a whole new sensual world.

- Prepare a bath for each other in turns or stir up the romantic universe by sharing a bath together. A cool bath is stimulating but it's best going for warm water as it comes highly recommended for relaxation and generating warm feelings. So, ensure you check the water temperature.

- Play music (A beautiful romantic rhythm and blues always works) in the background.

- Buy and use specially scented soaps, bathing oils and soft brushes. Most supermarkets have segregated sections for bath items. Go out and get the best for you with your partner in mind also.

- Set up an exit with a mat, a cozy bathrobe and large soft towel. Isolate the latter two items from whatever you use daily to make the experience special.

The Bathing Tantric Rite

You probably take a quick shower or get into the bathtub after a stressful day to get sex ready. But can you go back in time and recollect, when last you were in a web of lengthy memorable love with your partner in the bath? Conscious showering and washing together is an important part of tantric sex. Spending time in the tub is way beyond getting clean, it also is aimed at helping you:

- Enjoy the moment of being together in the water
- Allow body contact and stay in touch
- Bring to life your sensations
- Create your consciousness of each other

The most essential part of tantric bathing is to make washing each other a rite, done with an elevated consciousness. Instead of rubbing soap swiftly over body parts, focus steadily on certain spots. Be innovative while you do it, soapy hands offer a great platform to slide your hands over the skin of your partner. Apply different touches and different angles to delight the skin, from lengthy, smooth strokes to circular tracing around those delicate areas like the buttocks. Switch your touches, utilizing the soapy palms of your hands and light fingernails scratches on the arms and legs.

Begin with the nonsexual areas to create an eagerness for more sexual parts. Trace around the boobs and chest consciously, and into the inner thighs. Hands slipping delicately onto the more sensual areas. Washing in the private parts can a sort of new experience for the couples. Clean with an aura of innocence, still with the intention of stimulating your partner by adding a spice of teasing and tempting.

THE GOD AND GODDESS COSTUMING

Costuming as kids was always fun for everyone, especially when you got dressed up as your favorite superhero or heroine or probably costumed to look like your dream profession. But as we grew up, we became choosier and more cautious about attires. On your tantra date, unleash the freedom dressing beast and allow yourself have fun once again, play around with fabrics and styling. Choose clothes you never pictured yourself everyday wearing or utilize the one in your closet you had been saving for a special occasion (Don't you feel this a special occasion too).

Definitely, you like to think you will get loved for exactly who you are rather than what you portray via your outfits or what you look like. Of course, your inner being is the main centre of attraction in tantric lovemaking but beautifying your outer being is a show of respect for your person and your lover.

Most men swiftly get to the stage of nudity in lovemaking, but tantric sex involves being clad before going unclad. Cladding to seduce your partner and feeling good about yourself is an act of meditation that drags attention to your body, to put you in the mood of seduction and for open fun. Open yourself up to creativity, adhering to these effective suggestions:

- Tantric encouraging attires are usually of loose fitting and transparent, to blend with the flowing feel. Putting on sensual appealing fabrics such as *silk* encourages touch. Women are free to wear flowing dresses or beaded collars, the more revealing, the more enticing and pleasing to eye you become, the more inviting you are for touching. The man is permitted to wear a silk shirt (with the highest buttons open), silk boxers or cotton slacks. A tantric drilled man is not afraid to wear outfits commonly worn on the exotic islands called the *Pareos*, they are skirt like but quite masculine.

- Ensure these attires are unique, not your similar daily outfits.

- The cladding doesn't matter, as long as you feel good in them and brings delight to your partner.

- Wear an attention seeking jewelry that drags attention way more than your normal outing jewelry. Be striking in appearance, allow pearl strings dangle into your cleavage. Go for more lengthy earrings or thin belt twisted around your waist. You can add an extra spice by wearing ankle bracelets.

- Play around with recent styles of cladding you never had thoughts of ever wearing. Choose an attitude that allows you room to explore.

- Utilize colors. Tantric traditional colors are Red and

Purple. Colors go a long way in setting up a distinct sexual atmosphere. Wearing an orange underwear triggers the sexual center, a yellow scarf around the waist boosts your power, a purple shirt inspires you in achieving a more spiritual state of mind and bonding.

Allow yourself undress enticingly for your partner, put up your best strip show. Or undress each other simultaneously as slow and seductive as possible or rip off each other's clothes in a moment of intense passion.

THE PERFECT ROMANCE SET

Picture a movie setting for the most romantic movie ever imagined. How does this set look like in your mind? Have you ever wondered if you and your partner share the same picturesque of an ideal lovemaking space? It's essential you discuss your different ideas on a perfect set for lovemaking.

BUILD YOUR SET ASIDE LOVEMAKING AREA

Picture one of the classiest cathedrals you have ever been in. Think of replicating the classy nature in your lovemaking area, preparing the area meticulously.

Dressing your lovemaking area is so similar to dressing up yourself in many ways. Just as you dressed up in nice outfits, dress your room to its best. You could follow these tips:

- ➢ Lit the whole room with candles strategically positioned.
- ➢ Add a nice different scent to the room without going overboard probably with some fresh flowers or Aromatic room oils.
- ➢ Get a new bed covering and dress you bed beautifully.
- ➢ Get massage oils. They will likely come in handy at one point
- ➢ Get your bed taste buds stimulants which could include chocolate coated strawberry or chilled champagne.
- ➢ Clear every mess and put everything in their right places to avoid the area looking messy.

TILT YOUR SET

Try to be expressively creative when making love. Make love at a variety of places, indoors or outdoors. Things will fall into place beautifully when you bond together with a blessed intention and spiritual union.

But it's still a pretty good idea sticking to your same lovemaking set as it heightens the energy build up and enhances your union once you in that area.

THE RIGHT MUSIC CHOICE

Certain type of songs strikes a chord and penetrates the soul. Researchers have confirmed specific sounds, beats and tempo play a large role in dictating our breathing pattern and heart rate. It becomes more lucid that music is an essential on a tantric date. Make the right music choice and watch as you and lover bask in the moment with enjoyment, it could be classical, R n B or Hip Hop. Your music selection should be solely determined by the mood set you wish to trigger

THE ALTAR CONSTRUCTION

An altar is a designated space crafted out to keep what you hold dear and sacred, it could also be a representative symbol for prayers. Get sacred objects you cherish, which inspire you to higher levels of consciousness. Decorate the house with those sacred objects to give it a spiritual feel when you take a look at them. These decorations should be done collectively with your partner, it is a bonding experience.

Before making love, you both approach the altar to say a word of prayer in silence or aloud. The items on your altar could include your pictures or that of your respected leaders, candles, water, air, flowers or sacred objects.

RITES TO HONOUR TO MAKE YOUR SPACE HOLY

The rites of love involve motion and dedication that help craft a space of safety and a holy area where you can easily surrender to each other. Here you get transformed and also get into a trance like state that leads to intense pleasure. These are ways to sanctify your unique area:

- Walk around the area in each corner saying prayers of dedication
- Share a gift with each other as an offering of your love and devotion

CALM THE MIND

Balance into your space after a bath and adhere honorably to the rites of the area and calm the mind to grant permission for energies mixing. Sit up with doing the eye gazing and breathing techniques. Say a chant to align your energy while calming the mind.

PLAN YOUR ACTIONS TOGETHER

It's so normal in the average sex life of a couple that they just go into the sexual action quietly. But tantric sex says no to sex this way since it is practice of dedication and not an unconscious action. Take time to sit opposite each other and plan your actions during lovemaking together. The energy of sex and love is a powerfully driven energy. Open up on what you would love to show or carry out during love making and it will very much likely happen as you allow energy expand and blend. In turns, pour out your heart on the matter allowing your every need come up. Freely ask of your partner what you need.

Note:

Even with a full schedule for work or other commitments always craft out time for you and your partner. Set up for lovemaking and create a sensual oriented bathing ritual. Dress up keenly, for your special occasions and don't forget to make holy your body and space with rites cleansing and prayers.

CHAPTER ELEVEN: DRILLS FOR THE LOVE TO ATTAIN BEATITUDE

In this chapter you know and learn:

- How to reach the level of beatitude

- Plain drills that aid alignment of your energy

- Triggering your senses and partner stimulation

- To find what triggers your tantric love

- Learn sex in the flow lane

- The rites that make lovemaking special

Now the platform for tantra connection has been set, what do you do? A natural answer should come but as tantra is a practice rite, some activities could be done together to aid your pleasure and aid you attain higher levels of beatitude

WHAT IS BEATITUDE?

Have you ever been so happy beyond words could explain?

Now that's a state of beatitude deeper than the normal delightful feeling, juicier than any other joyful moment. In that moment it all seems perfect, Beatitude is the greatest level of happiness. It is almost like a taste heaven on earth. Beatitude implies you feel so good and every cell in your body gets triggered.

Getting to a level of beatitude is dependent on how you breathe, channel your energy, feel love and do drills in that very moment. This process involves you activating and integrating your mind, body and soul. By doing this you are moving from a level of survival to level of rendering service, from a level of pleasure to another level of creativity and moving from control to a level of total surrender. It works effectively.

ALIGNING YOUR ENERGY

Life isn't always as we planned and each individual with their own differing stress period. Hence, it is not always expected you and your lover will particularly always be in the same mood or on the same wavelength, it is very essential before the start of any tantric practice that you do as much as you can to align yourselves on the same wavelength and create a levelled love ground.

One of the most effectively tested and trusted ways to align your energy is by breathing together. This breathing exercise can be carried out in different postures with the aim of achieving fresh sensations. Sit backing each other and take full breaths exhaling and inhaling together. It helps build a connection with each other.

JUST KEEP YOUR GAZE ON ME: LOOK DEEP IN MY EYES

Gazing into a partner eyes is a foundational tantric sex drill, it leads to more enhanced experiences once it is done the right way. It comes across as simple just gazing at each other but it's actually difficult focusing your eyes on an individual for some time. Intimate fears make it even more discomforting to carry out. How do you feel when we you look into the depths of the eyes of your lover? Probably you felt delighted, or at other times felt vulnerable, conscious of yourself or probably it was even the most embarrassing moment you ever experienced. But they are normal feelings.

Eye gazing helps still the mind and helps refocus your attention. This sort of gives your partner a sense of delight that you are there for him or her, which is a good impression. It helps you confront your fears and ends up transforming your relationship for the best.

The first time most individuals fell in love, they really spent a lengthy period of time looking in each other's eyes but after some time that reduces either consciously or unconsciously. Eye gazing by tantric standards helps in recreating the awesome experience of when you first fell in love.

Eye gazing can be carried out in an upright position facing your partner in a comfortable relaxing but open posture and look kindly into each other's eyes for at least 3 minutes. This can also be done in a yab yum position. Keep in mind you are in no staring competition, so keep your eyes very relaxed and allow yourself blink when you need to. Keep yourself open to observe and appreciate the beauty and joy exuded in your lover's eyes. If ever you feel any discomfort doing this, just keep doing it. You will observe you later become more calmer while carrying it out.

THE ESSENCE OF THE HEART HOLD

This drill channels love energy through your hands and into the other's heart. Position your right hand over your lover's heart. Simultaneously, let your partner place his/her right hand over your heart. This helps send out love energy through your heart down to your arm and into your lover.

THE LOVER PASSION BUD

Being wrapped in your lover's arm brings about a certain sense of security, comfortability and excitement as if adrenaline driven. Tantric drills encourage bonding between partners in all sort of postures and situations. When carrying this out, the partners approach each other steadily eyes fixed and bodies float into each other while embracing each other comfortably. Breathe in alignment slowly breathing in and breathing out. As you breathe, allow your bodies melt into each other. Stay this way for as long as you desire. While separating, set yourself apart slowly maintaining eye contact.

SENSE STIMULATION TRIGGER

All senses are given their due honor and care when making

love the tantric way. This implies all organs senses oriented are involved and functioning as they are centers of the body. Here are some exercises that can be done:

The Mouth and Face: With your fingertips trace around your lover's mouth and pulling the lips apart softly. Sucking on the lips are sexual organ stimulating. Extend your touch towards the area around the mouth then cheeks and then the face. Get a blindfold around your lover eyes and feed him or her probably strawberry or ice-cream.

The Eyes: They are the windows to the soul. Touch around your partner eyes softly, then gaze into his or her eyes then downwards towards other parts.

The Nose: A cherished organ in tantra drills especially for the breathing drills. It's function to perceive scent comes in handy during love making. Stimulate your partner sense of smell by wearing him or her a blindfold and passing various scents under his or her nose. Allow each other sniff your bodies just like animals do with no holding back. Then only your fingers go through your bodies stimulating you with sweet sensations

The Hands: Touch has proven overtime to possess healing effects as seen via massages. In turns, you become a receiver and at another time the giver. Vibe the energy of your lover's hand you are holding and that of your own hand just so you can identify the varying sensation of touching and being touched. Inhale and exhale deeply sending the right energy through your hands and go adventurous with your partners hand by exploring. Feel its differing texture (the soft palms or the hardened fingernails). Give each other a feedback on what you feel.

The Ears: This part is quite ignored when it comes to relating to sexual impulses but this is a very erotic part of the body. Put your thumbs into the ear openings, pressing on around the inner skin. Stretch and drag know the earlobes (they can handle the pressure) and around the outer ear. Whisper sweet nonsense in your lover's ear. Sing a song expressively into your partner ears. Music is truly essential in your tantric drills.

DISCOVERING YOUR TANTRIC LOVE STIMULANT

Do you view your relationship as sacred? Do you hold it in the highest esteem? Until you do, you can never get the best out of your relationship. Take time out to reflect on your relationship with awe and handle it with the highest respect. Infuse into your relationship words or emblems unique to you both. A certain couple tantric triggers happen to be the depiction of a dragon and phoenix. Another couple tantric trigger is the picture of two birds with beaks entangled. Find an emblem that triggers both of you.

THE FLOW LANE FOR SEX

Tantric Sex demands from you an awareness to every sensation but sometimes we are carried away with the action that we don't really feel any sensations. Start by sitting or standing together with eyes shut while making low sounds and staying calm until you are motivated to put yourself in motion.

Body Exploration the Advanced Way

There lies hidden an endless clandestine in your body edifice which can only be uncovered via tantric practices either solely or with your partner. Don't be ashamed to reveal yourself. Even if you have been into lovemaking for a long time or carrying out tantric drills. Your partner genitals are still a mystery in need of solving. It is necessary you both give yourselves room to explore further.

CHAPTER TWELVE: BREACHING THROUGH OBSTACLES TO BEATITUDE

In this chapter we will know and learn:

- How past issues interfere with your tantric sex practice and your life as a whole
- The essence of dedicating time to be together
- To release intense emotions
- Getting over past desperation, obsession and anxieties
- How to strike a balance between male and female energies
- The right lifestyle to keep you healthy

As you move further on life journey, a time comes when you need to discover yourself, improve yourself or your spiritual levels, and then you tend to find out a whole lot of exciting things about yourself and the world at large. As you try to change certain things about yourself, lifestyle and relationships obstacles will definitely arise.

WHEN IMMENSE EMOTIONS FORCEFULLY COME THROUGH

One of the most powerful forces ever known is *Sexuality*, and these tantric sex drills aid generation of extreme sexual arousal. This could result in you having to face your previously suppressed problems. It can be quite fear triggering when hurting feelings stirr up again impromptu, but what's necessary is handling it the right way when it comes. Try resolving it so you don't have to live in that fear anymore. Tantric practices help in these emotional releases.

Crafting Out Time For Your Loved One

Most couples complain about lack of time for sex. Of a truth, everyone is busy and tend to push some things high on the priority list and others at the bottom of that list. Hence, it is important to find drills that can realistically be done together to enable the energy flowing in between you. Here are some simple practices which could be done.

Partner's Morning Showers of Blessing

It is highly recommended you carry out this morning drill routinely before getting dressed up to start your day. Start by sitting on your knees facing each other. Bow before each other with hands shaped as in a praying posture. Take about 10 belly depth breaths in unison, first 5 with eyes shut and second 5 making eye contact with your partner. In turns, saying words of blessings to each other. Speak sweet and sincere words to yourselves.

After saying the blessing, take 3 more breaths still ensuring you keep eyes in contact, then take a bow, hug and kiss.

Connection for 10 minutes

Am exercise connection for 10 minutes can be carried out. Here's how:

- **A connection for 10 minutes:** Set aside a time during the day or night to lie together for just 10 minutes. Most advisable nights. The essence is to feel each other energy.

- **Sharing for 10 minutes**: Give details about how you day went, how you feel. Just basically say what's on your mind. Similar to just letting go and letting your partner share those moments with you.

- **The Acknowledgement for 10 minutes**: Dedicate time to be open with each other on what you like and appreciate about your partner. Recognition has an effect on your lover and basically humans as a whole. It brings about a sense of love and purpose, it makes you full of life.

Redirecting Your Anger

It is almost unavoidable that you won't get angered by either the words or actions of your partner. But rather than building up that anger from deep within tantra profers a better solution. *The Lion's play* is a method tried and trusted to help you redirect your anger. Put your hands together while roaring loudly as a lion would , and push on each other's hands with strength equality . It might sound foolish, but it definitely works. After a few minutes of action even the most doubtful of the both of you will likely begin laughing. Keep doing this until you can see yourself and your partner both laughing and see the anger dissolve.

Getting Over Separation

Tantra dwells so much on the power of connection therefore, when you feel little to excruciating pain or probably feel a hindering block during the progress of your drills, you are probably tasting some extent of separation. You could feel Self isolation like you are separated from your own self, or separated from your loved one, separated from your work, separated from your family or from the world as a whole; you may likely know the distorting feeling of isolation from not belonging in a clique or group. Tantric practices help in filling the gap created by separation by opening your heart.

Just imagine moments you have built up a feeling of separation on your own maybe by: judging yourself, judging others, or having unattainable expectations. Try to sit with your partner facing each other and say words like these: "I feel isolated from you when I ..."; and then say, "I feel in tune with you when I ….." or This gets me in touch with your feelings. Doing these strengthens your choice and enables you to choose whatever moment you want. Either to stay separate or stay together.

STRIKING THE MASCULINE AND FEMININE ENERGY BALANCE

Sometimes imbalance of energies builds up tension and feelings of incompatibility in between couples. Uniting energies as a couple is quite essential.

The Six Directives to Bring About Energy Equality

Nostril Breathing: You can control the balance your sexual energies by choosing which of the nostrils to block and which to open. To trigger more masculine energy, obstruct your left nostril and breathe only through the right nostril. To trigger more feminine energy, obstruct your right nostril and breathe only from the left nostril. You could also tilt your head to the left to generate more masculine energy or tilt to the right to generate more feminine energy.

Nostril Breathing Alternately: This is a popular drill in most yoga tutorials. Sit silently while putting your right index finger on your third eye and rest your thumb and middle finger on your nostrils. Breathe out forcefully and then obstruct one nostril with your finger and breathe out via the other nostril up to the count of seven. Then close that nostril while freeing the other nostril and breathe through the open nostril to the count of seven. Without halting, keep doing this alternately closing and opening the nostrils as you breathe.

Utilizing varying sounds: Chant "om" to trigger more masculine energy and "aum" to trigger more feminine energy. Then say the two sounds switching them at intervals for a lengthy period of time till you feel the sounds blend.

Walk around in his or her shoes: Try walking as a male if you are a female, or try walking as the female if you are a guy. This is always bringing about funny feedbacks and reactions. That's the beauty about it.

Pay Attention To Colors: It helps when you understand the power of colors in relation to sexuality. Masculine energy is normally cool blue, and the feminine energy is always a color which represents emotions and passion which is mostly red, surround yourself with either color. Redirect your attention on either red or blue, by gazing at an item identified red or blue, or deliberately put on a red or blue cladding.

Put Your Body In Motion: To drag in more masculine energy, take your hands out from your sides, over your head and into the sky; gazing up, picture pulling in energy from the sky. To pull in more feminine energy, tilt downwards slightly as if trying to pull energy up from earth and into channel it to your heart.

HANDLING FRUSTRATION OF WHO GOES ON TOP

A whole lot of relationships circle around battles of control. Based on tantric terms the center for control lies in the third chakra. In bringing about solution to battle control relationship, do drills related to your center. Place your hand on your power center while doing the drills. You could gaze in your partner's eyes as your partner does same too, then place your left hand on your power center with the intention of receiving more power. Just breathe, after which you take your right hand high and out to your partner as a gesture that portrays your power expression and right to be heard.

OVERCOMING HOPELESSNESS AND ATTACHMENTS

A necessary function of any spiritual path you have chosen is to help you reach a state where you are no longer attached to anyone or in most cases anything. The feeling of desperation or clinging nature to your partner may feel all too familiar. For some, it pushed all their past lovers away from them as they were always viewed as extremely needy. One way, that works so effectively in resolving this feeling of desperation is a built understanding about it.

Reminisce a bit, take a throwback to your past with your parents just to see whether you were abandoned (and still feel you were the reason they left you) or suffocated you (so you felt used). These actions can make you push away intimacy, basically you scared of having to go through abandonment or suffocation all over again. Besides getting to understand, the following two tantric practices might help:

- Breathe deeply whenever you feel needy, before you carrying out an action or say words that grasps at someone, take a deep breath, letting the sound come out loud enough as you breathe out. Allow energy surges, to and fro your body.

- Feel yourself rooted to a floor. Stand with feet conveniently set aside and tilt your knees slightly downwards. Bounce up and down (be careful not to mount pressure on your knees!), taking deep breaths that go into your first chakra center which symbolizes security.

RIDDING FRIGHT AND OBSESSIONS

Possession of fears and anxieties from the inside can trigger panic attacks, and constantly distorting thoughts that become obsessions, which are not only disturbing but take your attention, making you absent minded in a moment. Tantric practices demand you to always be present in whatever moment. Overcoming this, requires you to create being present and achieving this, demands you utilize the two drills in the previous section on overcoming hopelessness and attachment. Other breathing drills also come in handy too, like breathing out for a longer space of time than when you breathing in. Focus on whatever lies presently in the moment. Quiz yourself, "What is present now? " When you find yourself worrying about the past or bothered about what lies hidden in the future, still keep quizzing yourself "What is present now".

Note:

You can also clear mental obstacles by working on your nutrition and wellness by watching eating habits. Try to imbibe the right kind of dieting.

CHAPTER THIRTEEN: FITNESS AS A COUPLE FOR TANTRIC SEX

In this chapter you will get learn and know:

- How doing drills together aid the pumping of the love muscles
- The right yoga to carry out together
- Drills that affect your sex energy
- How emotional issues are worked through in a workout

Previously, you learnt about the important role being fit physically plays in pleasurable sex. Your body is your edifice of love but now you are readier to share it with your partner.

Go through the steps in previous chapters pertaining to couples and do them with your partner. Here, you'll get to learn more physical drills and motion you can carry out together to honor and respect your body.

THE ESSENCE OF DOING PHYSICAL DRILLS TOGETHER

It is proven by worldwide researchers that exercising brings about intensified sexual arousal. Physical drills are energy triggering which is important for sex and forces you to focus on your body, helping you acquire sensual awareness while also building up your strength and stamina during different sexual positions. It also distributes chemicals of pleasure to the brain. Working out with you partner enables chemicals such as Endorphin also known as the Love chemical and Oxytocin also known as Cuddle chemical flow right through your body. Giving you assurance for definite pleasure to show love during sex.

DANCING AS A WORKOUT

It is so amazing watching people dance but even more fun when you try dancing yourself. While caught up in the excitement of swaying to every beat at its own tempo, you are carrying out one of the greatest workouts of all time.

Dancing is a wonderful drill that works on all kinds of muscles and sets your spirit free in the process. It is one of the most powerful ways to trigger your body in entirety and channel sexual energy through your body, even at certain points it serves as signals for orgasmic highs for both male and female. This makes the activity an extremely perfect warmup if you really want to get all interactive with your partner.

THE WHITE TANTRA ROUTINE: THE STEPS INVOLVED

Tantra generally refers to your personal practices, which could include the yoga poses which links to the Chakras or centers of energy. Anytime you strike a pose it triggers one or many of the chakras and the emotions connected to those centers. These yoga poses profit you by:

❖ Creating a foundational trust depth between you and your partner as you both need each other for the motions.

❖ Striking the right balance as you both require dependence on each other to adjust your physical balances while shifting in and out of a pose.

121

- ❖ Showing you the requirement of true cooperation, because without working together you will struggle to get in and out of poses together.
- ❖ Laying down an example on how you can communicate through your bodies. This aids you when you try to communicate emotionally.
- ❖ Allows you chance to be in support of one another while building up your physical strength
- ❖ Gives you room for laughter and fun

THE COUPLE'S CONNECTION

Begin the session by being present fully for one another, no distractions or side attraction. Sit facing one another, gazing in each other's eyes. Knees bent out, place feet conveniently in front of you, with your feet on the outside of your partner's. Wrap each other by stretching out your arms to cling to your partner conveniently on the sides or under the shoulder. Breathe out and breathe in together to align your energies. Do this for up to seven breaths or extend for longer periods if you so desire.

CELEBRATING BY CIRCLING AS A COUPLE

Lay on the floor opposite each other. Legs outstretched as distant as possible with feet making contact. Hold hands while one partner reaches out for the other, the other leans backwards. Carry this out again but in reverse. Breathe in as your partner breathes out. Create circles moving from left together, stretching your right side and then the opposite side. Change directions in the reverse. At intervals form small and bigger circles. Have fun.

STANDING FROM A SQUATTING POSITION

Aid yourselves into a squat position while grasping onto each other's wrists. Bounce softly, connecting to your lower energy centers as they get stimulated. Take a rise to a standing posture steadily, playing along as you balance one another.

THE COUPLE SHAPED COBRA

Lie fully stretched on your stomach with heads touching and hands underneath the shoulders while slowly lifting the upper body. Open your heart to one another and extend your neck and head upwards while arching backwards. Open up the throat chakra, this gives you enablement to utter true words in all sincerity to your partner. Go down and rise up again. Breathing in and breathing out at similar pace.

THE TABLE FORMED BY PARTNERS

This is an amazing experience for lovers. One partner goes on all fours, while keeping his back straight and shaped in form of a table which the other partner allows it. Swap roles is your weight permits it.

STRENGTHENING YOUR BODY IN BEDROOM

Yoga teachers across recommend bedroom body strengthening. And this can be carried out by:

- Stand facing each other in the shower or in the bedroom. Prep up by gazing into each other's eyes while rolling your head from shoulder to shoulder, and extending your upper body by leaning in one direction and then to the other.

- You and your lover then roll your arms and hips in

alignments while still facing each other, as if gazing in a mirror.

- Once you're both feeling really elated, the female partner can turn her back and stretch over as the male partner leads into her pelvis into and away from the body. This creates a momentary thrust for her which leads to working out in and around her hips and strengthens her thighs, and resistance for him to work out on the belly, thighs, arms and hips.

- In the partner involved push-ups the male lies on his back, raisin his hips in the air, thereby putting his lower back into action while working out the abs while she leans over him, supporting herself with straight arms and hands on the bed, lowering and lifting her body as if carrying out push-ups over him. This can also be done in reverse positions, with the man over the woman while he does the push-ups.

BOXING THE YOGA WAY

The workout begins with extensions that reach upward, picture extending for your strength and stretching to speak up. Many exercises are done in pairs, to simulate confrontation with a real partner, such as the tug of war, in which each holds an end of a rope, saying "yes" and "no" consequently in turns. After each drill, the partners share how they feel, and whether they were truly able to come true as strongly as they wanted. Who pulled the rope harder? Whose voice is more persuasive? The participants are invited to relate the drill with occurrences in their relationships in which they probably might have disagreed about even the tiniest and most unexpected things.

The motions and words of expression in Yoga boxing create a powerful bond between your sense of power and your throat, permitting energy for self-expression to flow with consummate ease to the sexual area. Yoga boxing seems to be working for others as well, with women as well as men. So next time you're extremely agree and won't go near your partner, grab a rope and engage your partner in a tug of war. With winner taking it all and enjoys the spoils of sex later.

CHAPTER FOURTEEN: ADVANCED TANTRA SEX STYLES AND TECHNIQUES

Tantric sex is all about having fun. The styles and techniques you have been reading in the above chapters are based on this view. Tantric sex helps you to create new pleasurable experiences in your relationship. Although Sex is treated as sacred, but tantra believes that it shouldn't be a boring experience. It is when you and your partner enjoy the sexual activity, that you can create and transfer energy. This is why several tantric sex practices has time for play. There are several ways you and your partner can play together, and some of them have been listed below. This section will cover fun ideas that you can practice with your partner during tantric sex playtime.

PLAY LIKE A CHILD

A child is the perfect image when it comes to playing without inhibitions. This is mainly because a child is always faced with several fun options to choose from when playing. We all had the child's fun attitude to life because we were all once children. However, the negative experiences, fears, responsibilities and restrictions we face while growing up had made us neglect these fun side. With Tantric sex play, it can be restored. Playing with your partner during sex is a good way of calming their fears and healing them of their negative experiences. When you allow play in your relationship, you are putting yourself in the position to imbibe those positive and fun child qualities.

THE IMPORTANCE OF PLAY IN SEX

Play has several benefits for both the physical and mental health of the individuals involved. Basically, it makes you happier, and according to a research, happier people are stronger and more immune than others. The research also found out that couples who are happy in their marriages lives and last longer than those that aren't so happy. We have explained in this eBook how smiling can help you and the society at large. One main way to achieve smiling is through playing. Playing during sex will greatly reduce the limitations between you and your lover and deepen your connection. It will also make your sex life thrilling and exciting.

POSITIVE AFFIRMATIONS TO IMPROVE SEX LIFE

Positive affirmations are important in everyday life. It is you consciously saying and deciding the positive outcome you want to get from your life, with no exception to sex. When you make and mean your affirmations, it makes it more possible to attain. Saying what you want loudly or writing it on a piece of paper helps you believe and work towards them better. Some affirmations you can use to improve your sexual life have been listed below. Read them aloud, inhale deeply when you say them and picture them coming into reality.

- I am happy with my sex life

- I find every moment of pleasure desirable

- I am in love with a god/goddess

- I deserve joy in my love making

- My partner gives me confidence during sex

LAUGHING AND YOUR OVERALL HEALTH

If smiling can greatly improve your health life, there are no boundaries to what laughing can do for you. Laughing gives you the similar benefits you get from smiling. It makes you younger and reduce wrinkles on your face as you grow up. It improves your immune system and overall physical and mental health. Laughing can change your mood and energy positively in a matter of seconds. Laughing can open you up for more love, which is the main objective of tantra. Laughing more with your partner will greatly reduce the physical and emotional tensions in your relationship.

DANCING FOR EACH OTHER

Dancing is an activity we engage in to relieve stress, but do you know it is a vital practice of love too? Dancing helps to transfer energy within you, to your partner. Tantric sex encourages that as part of playing, you and your partner should dance for each other. This will increase the love and connection between you. Before you start dancing, dim the lights, decide who will dance first and get proper outfits for the occasion. However, the dancer gets to select his/her preferred music, and the outfit you put on must be sexy to your partner. Dance swiftly and let your body move with the rhythm of the song.

While dancing, you have to let go of your self-consciousness and image or underlying thoughts like not being able to dance or feeling stupid. Instead ignore these thoughts and focus on the satisfaction and eyes of your partner. When your partner is dancing, do not make jest of him/her, concentrate and let your feelings show that you appreciate the effort.

FEASTING ON YOUR LOVE

Another way you can spark up passion in your relationship is through the use of food. This involves the way you buy your food, where you eat them and how you eat them with your partner. Increasing love through food starts from buying and cooking together with your partner, which can be termed food foreplay. However Tantric sex raises the use of food to a whole new level in which you make your partner the table while you feed on him/her and vice versa.

TOYS FOR TANTRIC PLAY

The best toy you can have in tantric sex practices is your sense of imagination, your body parts, soul and your partner. However tantric sex does not limit your choice of toys to these things, rather there are several real toys you can use to make tantric sex more fun. Tantric sex approved toys are different from any love aids or sex toys because of their special requirements.

A tantric sex toy should be able to;

- Increase connection between you and your partner

- Increase excitement and calmness

- Shouldn't let you lose focus or concentration on the main goal

- Help you achieve greater bliss and fun

- Help fasten the process of releasing energy through your chakra channels.

Examples of tantric sex toys include Crystal onyx massage egg and Crystal wand. These two toys help to stimulate and excite you and your partner's body parts

PART 5

THE JOURNEY TO A BLISSFUL TANTRA RELATIONSHIP.

Our love life is a very important part of our existence. So many people daydream about having a perfect love life. Many of us can't wait for the day that we meet "our soul mate", the one and only person destined for us, the one who really gets us. However, many of us don't seem to get that " perfect soulmate". We end up in relationships that sooner or later becomes a heart ache for us. Many get depressed as a result of their relationships. As a matter of fact, many give up on love altogether and decide to live a life of solitude. This is where the Tantra method of a relationship comes into place.

The idea of Tantra brings about sex. This is because tantra deals with the sexual energy between two individuals. Tantra itself talks about how sexual energy could be used to feel more love in the heart. However, let it be understood that tantra is not all about sex or else we won't be talking about how to maintain a blissful love relationship following the tantra style.

A tantra relationship is all about an energetic and spiritual contact between two individuals. The relationship itself is not for mere physical or genital stimulation and enjoyment but to connect emotionally and spiritually with others. But how do we do this. How do we find the perfect soulmate using the Tantra style? How do we know when we have a spiritual connection with a potential love partner? And most of all how do we maintain the relationship that we have built with the perfect tantra soulmate? No need for loneliness and heartaches anymore because this chapter might be all it takes to help you fall in love and discover your perfect tantra partner. This chapter would be divided into two sections that would have subtopics under them. The first section would be based on how a person could start by initiating the ideal tantra lifestyle and how it can be used to create lasting relationships. The second section would be based on the

Tantra married couples and how they can have a "very happily married life", using some basic tantra techniques and tricks.

CHAPTER FIFTEEN: INITIATING THE TANTRA LIFESTYLE; A BASIC GUIDE TO CREATING A BEAUTIFUL LOVE STORY

WHILE YOU ARE STILL SINGLE.

One has to understand that in the path to finding a "true tantra soulmate", love has to come from within. This simply means that you cannot truly be with a partner if you don't appreciate yourself. First things first, you need to first fall in love with yourself before you can fall in love with another. Many people easily get depressed in their love relationship and they often find themselves in conflict with their partner because they feel a sense of unworthiness within themselves. Look at it this way, some people try to depend on others for their happiness. You would hear them often say that they are looking for their "better half" or that they need someone who would complete them. Some even believe that their lives can make no meaning until their "better half" comes into the picture.

These set of people would expect that the love partner they find must be perfect, never default of positive characters and always willing to give them maximum attention. Because they do not feel themselves to be truly worthy, their happiness then depends on their partner. They feel so insecure about themselves that they would want their partner to constantly make declarations of love to them. However, as a result of their insecurities they would hardly be truly happy and contented with their love relationships.

In a tantra journey, one first has to create a sense of wholeness within the self. You have to understand that being single does not mean you are not complete. There is no such thing as a better half. You are your better half so fall in love with yourself!!! Look at yourself in the mirror and appreciate all the qualities that you have both internal and external. Learn to get absorbed in yourself. Take yourself out on a treat, as you would normally have done if you had gone out with a date. Look pretty or charming for yourself. You do not have to wait for someone to tell you that you look good before you tell yourself. When we truly love ourselves, we become happy from within. Remember, you are that special someone and the more you practice loving yourself the more you create a loving atmosphere around yourself. Build yourself up!!! Stop thinking constantly of that "imaginary love partner", instead get absorbed in your own world.

Engage yourself totally on the things that you love doing, who knows, someone might be around the corner secretly admiring you while you are enjoying those activities that you are doing. So many people are often attracted to those who surround themselves with the things they love.

Remember, a tantra relationship should often emphasize on a deep level of emotional and spiritual connection and if you are not able to sort yourself out first, then not only would you become emotionally unstable but you would not also truly connect with a partner.

LET THE HUNTING BEGIN.

Since Tantra is mostly about making a spiritual connection with another, the hunt for the soulmate should be something " more flowery, respectful, honouring" and not just some sort of "hook up". Tantra deals with conscious loving, so one has to be deliberate in the actions towards another.

Meaning that you must be interested in really studying and knowing that person. You have to understand that in any kind of love relationship, friendship is key. You need to develop a deep trusting and intimate friendship towards that person. It is this friendship that ignites a spiritual connection leading to the heightening of the sexual energy between you and your potential tantra mate.

Understand that some sort of " flirting" has to first take place before a connection is made. In making your move towards that potential mate, you have to be patient and to learn how to take your time. As a guy, you have to understand that when you flirt you do not do it to feel good about yourself. You are trying to make a friend out of that person and not to make a score. Mind your behavior, most tantra partners want a nice guy and not someone who is trying to prove that they are not just cool, but also a "bad ass. In the tantra path, we have to be careful and respectful when it comes to other people's boundaries.

These things should be done by will, you can't assert your own demands on the person you are flirting with. For instance, a man could ask outrightly what a woman wants. He should try to ask her about the day and time that going out on a date would be convenient for her. He could also ask her of the time it would be okay for him to call her. These things should be done ever so carefully and consciously. But then one other thing that should be noted when flirting with someone is that we shouldn't try to act like someone we are not. Remember that it is who we are that matters and not what we are.

HOW CAN YOU DETECT THE RIGHT PERSON FOR YOU?

Tantra deals with spiritual attraction this means that one has to look beyond the physical qualities of a potential partner. Truth be told, one way or the other we all imagine our perfect soulmate to be someone of very intense physical attraction. Most ladies would always dream about that very tall, dark and handsome guy with piercing and intimidating eyes, however as time goes on and with a clearer understanding of tantra, the whole idea of the "perfect mate" completely changes. The basic aim of tantra is to look beyond the physical being to see and connect with the inner soul of the "potential love partner".

You have to erase all forms of stereotypes of how you want the ideal partner to be. Forget about the country the person might have come from, forget about the race, age, religion and culture and focus on the inner qualities of that individual. Do not join the " group " that always talk about having a "Type" when it comes to love partners. Infact, looking beyond the physical one can find new and unlimited number of love matches. Yes, aiming for the eyes really works. In practicing tantra you have to look into the eyes of the potential love partner to see the god/goddess within. This is because tantra practice believes that every person is a divine being with a divine nature and so should be viewed and treated as such.

In searching for the Tantra mate, you have to look deeply within the mind as to how you want that person to be. Ask yourself if you value physical qualities over the inner one. When you meet a potential tantra mate ask yourself, "is the person really nice?", is he or she one who would put your thoughts and wellbeing first? Do you think he or she can take very good care of you?

But also, apart from looking beyond their eyes, there are also other factors that could determine in detecting the right tantra partner. The main issue is, "Do both of you really agree on basic things that could make the relationship work? How committed do you want to get to that relationship? What are your contributions to making that relationship to work? The basic rule is that you can make " any" relationship to work if you really want it to work, that is, if you really set your mind at it no matter the obstacle that comes your way. If you both are really committed to getting along and you have enough love and respect for each other to work out any differences, then there is almost nothing that could stop the relationship from not working out.

PREPARING FOR A FRESH START WITH A TANTRIC PARTNER.

Before you enter into a new relationship, you have to clear up your conflicts with your past relationship. The mind is a very strong factor in almost every aspect of our lives and until we have fully cleared and prepared our minds against all doubts, one can't be fully ready for a new relationship. There are some things that some people believe in their minds about love and whether they admit it or not these people unconsciously sabotage their efforts of entering a new relationship. Are you amongst these set of people? What are the things that you believe about love that is hindering you from entering a new relationship? What kind of beliefs do you have about finding a Tantric Match? Now let us explore some of these beliefs;

One of the most common reasons why some people feel easily depressed and insecure when they think about relationships is because of the belief that even if they find someone, the love would soon turn sour. This is not always true. Some people think that love does not always last forever. However, one has to change the mind against these beliefs. Tantra teaches about conscious and deliberate loving. With deliberate steps through tantra one can learn how to love another. You have to understand that love should not depend on your feelings. If you set your mind at constantly loving someone, you would.

"Being in love is miserable. It makes one weak. It makes one vulnerable. Love distracts one from his/her focus in life". This not always have to be true. Infact, with the right tantric partner, this is not true at all. Your partner could become your greatest pillar of support. True love makes one stronger and not weak. Love produces happiness and when you are happy with yourself and your tantric partner then you should never feel miserable. One of the biggest believe and fear that people carry around regarding relationships is that having sex with your partner can ruin your relationship. Understand that love is not based on sex. Your values and your worth should not be determined by your body at all. A true tantric partner understands that a spiritual and emotional connection is the goal and not just the consummation of the physical body. But then the belief that sex destroys a relationship could actually affect a person's thoughts actions and behaviors that would then lead to the breakup of that relationship.

Other beliefs that might make you feel so unworthy of being in a romantic relationship is the idea that you will always get hurt in the end, you are better off being alone or rather "destined" to be alone. This is all untrue. All these thoughts stem out from one's personal experiences with past relationships. Your personal experience with a former relationship could make you ask and dwell on the question; " If it did not work out before, what difference can it make now?". Not everybody is the same so be positive, open your heart. Change these beliefs around and say it to yourself. Tell yourself that you are worthy of love and you can be spiritually and emotionally attached to someone. Your positive beliefs could bring about your true tantric partner so ask yourself, "How much are you really holding back?"

THE REAL DEAL IN A TANTRIC RELATIONSHIP.

In the introductory part of this chapter, it was mentioned that tantric sex is more than just sex. In tantric sex, the mind shifts to a whole new form of attraction, "a spiritual attraction". You have to understand that in practicing tantra, your body is a spiritual temple and you would not just anybody exploiting it. Infact, when you already understand that your body us not only a spiritual temple, but also special, you develop control and discipline with your body. You do not become loose and your sexual appetite is been restrained. Not that you shouldn't develop sexual energy towards another, but then you would understand that tantric sex is a very special and sacred thing between you and your tantric partner and should not be shared with anyone else.

In Tantric practice, you should look beyond the obvious (physical attraction or qualities) to the inner being.

Beyond material offerings, can your partner cope with your love and your flaws? We all desire someone who truly gets us and not just some " sex mate". Someone who we can be vulnerable around without having doubts, someone who we can lower our defensive walls when he/she is around. More than just this, both of you have to develop a "common language", you have to be on the same page. You have to support each other in all your affirmations and the paths that you both choose in life. You would have to learn to accept all parts of each other even in difficult situations. Treat each other with the utmost respect and honesty. When you and your partner choose to consciously and deliberately love each other against all odds, then both of you could even create " sex magic" together.

When you meet a potential "Tantra partner", how do you both feel that soul mate connection? Soo many people look for different signs that would show them that they have finally met their soul mate, however since a tantra relationship deals with a deep spiritual connection, how would you then know that you have finally meet your tantra soulmate.

Firstly, both of you would feel like you have known each other forever since the beginning of time. It might have been just a short while that you both met, but then meeting the person won't feel so strange, irrespective of the circumstances you both met. You might even feel that you have both shared past lives as lovers.

Secondly, one way or the other you would be able to sense what your mate feels or thinks before he or she talks. It's as if your thoughts and ideas are the same.

Thirdly, you feel peaceful and comfortable around this

person. You feel that there is no need to put your guards up around this person, because of that both of you are likely to get little or no feelings of doubt about your relationship. Also, because you both feel comfortable around each other, you get to know and appreciate each other on a deeper level.

However, in the hunt for a soulmate, do not close your mind around the belief that you are destined for just one soulmate. This is so not true. There is no such thing as a perfect someone for you. You can fall in love with more than just one person if only you put your mind to it, all it takes is just a spiritual connection. Tantra sex considers every human being as divine, so you can connect to someone's divinity and fall in love over and over again.

Take note of this. Just because you are incredibly attracted to someone does not make it a good match. How much does the person care for you? Is the person committed to being with you against all flaws and odds? Understand that lust and looks can be deceiving but that real energy between two people can be more lasting and genuine. Also understand that if the amount if energy, commitment and willingness you are putting in a relationship is not nearly what you are getting back, then you should back off, it is not worth it.

Lastly, understand that one should also practice safe sex when engaging in Tantra. Do not give the excuse that you are overlooking all other obstacles because of your spiritual connection with your partner. Your sexual health is also very important, do not joke with it. Tantric practice advises that you should always use "protective" if you are not so sure of your partner's sexual history and health. Take medical tests if necessary. All these things are very important for an effective tantra practice.

A ONE_SIDED TANTRIC RELATIONSHIP?

What if you practice the Tantra lifestyle or you want to start practicing the tantra relationship but your partner is not ready to do that? What if your partner, unlike you is not convinced about tantra practices? You do know that this might be a very great obstacle in your relationship and in attaining the perfect bliss, right? But then what steps can you take to solve this?

Yes, there are situations whereby a partner might be intrigued with the tantric lifestyle while the other is not. Most likely in situations like this it is that a partner got converted during the course of the relationship. After the conversion, the individual tells the partner about his/her experience but then the partner is not so thrilled for them to enter a tantric journey together.

If you find yourself in a situation like this, just be prepared for excuses from your partner. Your partner might want to express his/her views about why the Tantra path is not the right part in your relationship. Your partner might not be so comfortable about the sex positions and rituals that the tantra lifestyle offers. Your partner might not like the idea that tantra sex makes one feel so open and vulnerable. But then, you can also express your views about tantra sex to your partner. Help him/ her clear the myths that have been built around tantra sex. You can share books on tantra basic sex to your partner and why it is so important for an effective relationship lifestyle.

Explain that the goal of tantra sex is to open you both to more spiritual and emotional connection.

But what if your partner is not still convinced about it? You have to understand that it is okay if your partner decides not to follow the tantric path. You both can still have a very effective and blissful relationship if you both want to. Respect your partner's decision, but that does not mean you should stray from your tantric lifestyle. If your partner won't share the path with you then you have to go on the journey alone. You can still be in the relationship and do that. But how? One solution to this is that you can just bring home the love. Irrespective of your partner's path, share your tantric growth to him/her. Tantric lifestyle provides tutorial classes for its practices, so you can still share to your partner what you have learnt so far about it. You can still show him/her the immediate effect of your training, that is, the new-found sensitivity you've discovered, your spiritual depths, and loving way. All these can still be used to boost your relationship.

By engaging in the tantric lifestyle and even going to the

classes without your non-tantric partner you are creating more love and sexual energy that you can be able to take home to your partner at the end of the day. Your partner might not know so much about the practices or be convinced about it, but the energizing love effects that tantra brings to you might be enough to out a smile to his/ her face. But the thing is that no matter what you have to honor your partner. Do not engage in any tantric practices that are not in alignment with your relationship. Infact, study tantra with a practitioner who will honor, respect and support your relationship agreement. Do not engage in any sexual activity with another tantric practitioner if your non-tantric partner does not approve it.

But following the tantra journey alone can be quite tough sometimes. When you and your partner share different views, it can lead to a confrontation at times. Embrace it, and never blame your fights on tantra. In the long run, a partner might decide to leave because of your separate paths, as a result of the extreme sex technique that he/ she might not be able to cope with. Don't be heart broken. If you both found out you were incompatible, be glad. A basic tantra principle that you should learn is that "the love you have never leaves you even if particular people might"

THE IDEA AND ISSUES OF HAVING MORE THAN ONE TANTRIC PARTNER.

Many couples can decide to choose their own tantric rules, a couple can decide to be more accommodating to the idea of " polygamorous". It is simply the couple's decision. Polygamorous is simply the coming together of couples to form an intimate circle, it could involve intimate sexual activities. The thing is that the whole idea of tantric practices is to open couples to the love energy around them. So, if a couple decide to share their love energy to another, it is simply their choice. But this practice might not be easy at all because it could lead to couple's challenges in commitment and jealousy. Irrespective of its issues, some couples still find polygamorous as very satisfying for them.

What about the one that is not so satisfying, like a tantric sex affair? What if you are having a relationship with someone else that is beside your partner. Tantric sex affair has nothing to do with polygamorous, this is very different. On a general note having an affair with someone apart from your partner is when your partner has no knowledge and approval about it. In the tantric case, it can be very painful because of its association and promises to higher levels of eroticism. Therefore, betraying your partner or vice versa by having "deeper spiritual connections" with someone else. But how can this issue be contained?

People cheat for various reasons. It could be for the search of intimacy, commitment fears and even the fact that some people don't just want to remain monogamous. However, the situational can be evaluated. Most affairs arise from the illusion that someone outside the relationship has a more attractive energy than their partner. In a situation like this, the reason and intention for the affair has to be critically evaluated. You have to make some considerations about a tantric affair, like for instance are you or your partner involved romantically with someone else without having sex with them? If sex is involved, what kind of sexual activity? The most consideration to make is that is the affair worth it to end you and your partner's relationship?

The bottom line is that most affairs are initiated as a result of some breakdown in communication in a release. Couples should learn how to communicate their wants, sexual needs and its desires to each other. A person might learn to forgive his/her partner for sexual affair if a full understanding is made about why the person did it in the first place, and in most cases, it is as a result of a breach in communication. You should understand that any relationship can work out if both people want it to. A couple can heal from tantric love affairs if they both work at staying together. In other to avoid the experience of more sex affairs, you and your partner have to learn what to do to give your relationship an energy booster.

You have to learn how and when to be sensitive to each other. Learn to be a good listening partner, do not interrupt your partner when he/she is talking. If you have to lose weight, do it, take more tantra and even health classes if you have to. Know what your partner really wants by communicating constantly to him/her. Not every sex affair has to lead to a breakup, sort this issue out with your partner, if you want to. Communication solves a lot of problems amongst couples. Remember, the tantric lifestyle demands honesty. Be honest with each other no matter what!!!

CHAPTER SIXTEEN: HOLDING THE LOVE FOREVER; PRACTICING TANTRA FOR AN EVERLASTING MARRIAGE

THE PERFECT TANTRA COUPLE: TILL THE END OF YOUR DAYS?

So many couples do not end up happy after some time in marriage. The sexual love energy just fades away. Many resolves to divorce or breakaways. Some turn their affections to someone else, engaging in infidelity. While many if they decide to stay together do it for other reasons devoid of love. The question is; can love really last?

So many people desire a lifetime commitment that has more to do than just "settling down". Many couples today want a special kind of commitment that has to do with everything spiritual, emotional, psychological, physical and even material. But how can they achieve this? Can marrying for love really work?

Although many have doubted a positive answer to this last question posted above, but through the ages there have been improvements on the subject of love. People strive to attain sexual freedom, personal independence and prosperity. As each generation passes, people enter more blissful relationships than the last generation. Through the years, so many have tried to be conscious about love by going for therapies, seminars that addresses love issues and even tantra sex sessions to help in couples' sex lives. However, even with all the efforts made on finding love, some couples are still not able to attain a happily ever after married life. Let us explore the issues that deals with the love energy or lack of love in marriage and how couples can come to have an awakening in their love relationships.

Our psychological meanings to love could affect one 's love relationships. There are two dimensions of love, there is the "passionate love" and the "dispassionate one". So many strive for the former, some even get it at first but then it turns into a dispassionate relationship. When two Individuals meet themselves, they become overwhelmed by love, they feel this strong spiritual connection, this magnetic glow that attracts both individuals together. But then what happens? Why does this once passionate love fade away?

You have to understand that passion results from some kind of energy. A strong passionate love depends on energy for its survival. When two individuals first enter a relationship, it's always like an adventure. All they can think about is their "newfound lover", so they expend all their energy trying to impress and attract that other person. But sooner or later, this surge of energy wears off.

This new-found energy disintegrates mainly because of the "familiarity" that develops between both individuals. As a result of this both partners stop concentrating on each other, they then direct all their energy to other areas of their lives. In the process they lose their sexual energy for each other and develop just respect and appreciation for themselves. But is this enough?

As a married couple, one has to make time to constantly

make love to the partner. Constantly engaging in various sexual energy with the partner keeps the love energy strong between them. However, in keeping a strong love and passionate energy between the married couple more than just sexual activities is required. A constant love energy also needs its conscious efforts and maintenance because no forever love relationship is self-sustainable. A relationship is like a plant that when not constantly watered and cared for, could seriously deteriorate.

Communication is one of the key factors that keeps the love and sexual energy in a relationship together. But then many people are afraid or too shy to communicate with their partners because they feel that if they communicate their needs it might be rejected or that their partners might find them too needy. Holding down thoughts and ideas from one's partner boils down to pent-up frustration that could affect both partners in the long run.

In a relationship that involves effective communication, one has to recognize the differences between a man and a woman. Unity in a love relationship stands for wholeness.

However, many people mistake this concept of unity for "sameness". We have to understand that tantric practice is based on the "Yin/Yang theory". In the sense that it is the differences between a man and woman that brings about the combined success and wholeness of that relationship. Not differences that necessarily has to do with goals, dreams, interests, attitude towards life and so on. No, not that kind, but the sexual differences that actually distinguishes male from female. One can't have a satisfying passionate relationship without referring to these differences.

You see, these differences in the sexual nature is complementary. Both love partners need to work it to their advantage and that of their relationship. By embracing these differences and not condemning them, both partners can understand that for instance what a woman lacks, a man can do and vice versa.

In every relationship, although partners might share similar goals, interests and even psychologically they might be intertwined. But when it comes to sexual needs, in most cases each partner has his/her own different needs and views. This is because of the differences in the sexual nature between man and a woman. For instance, a woman's meaning for "Intimacy" might mean an entirely different thing for the man. In sex a woman craves this kind of "intimacy". For her it is more than just physical or genital satisfaction. She craves that closeness, a sort of communication that goes beyond the physical. Once that intimacy is removed from sexual activities, the woman becomes less aroused, less exercised and less energized towards sex. She ends up feeling unsatisfied and the more she does, the more the sexual energy and eventually the whole relationship becomes one with "dispassionate love". This is why tantric sex provides all sorts of methods and moves that a man and woman can use to attain maximum pleasure, bringing the sort of intimacy that the woman might need.

Love thrives through maintenance. Some people carry the idea that " if the love is real and divine, then it would automatically last forever, with not so much effort at trying to sustain it". However, the love energy needs to be continually charged and it can only be done using practical methods.

THE COUPLE'S HARMONY; RECONCILING THE DIFFERENCES (1)

In the last topic we briefly grazed on the subject of couple's intimacy and how it can be achieved through reconciling the differences between the man and the woman. When we mean "sexual differences" and "intimacy" this does not mean that the intimacy between the man and woman should be only displayed in sexual activities. The different sexual nature of the man and woman defines all other parts of the relationship.

Naturally, the male nature is different from the female's that is why there is the concept of Yin/Yang elements. Ideally, the male nature stands for positiveness, extroversion, light and heat. While that of the female is introversion, darkness, coolness, receptiveness, extra intuitiveness and accommodating. The tantric aim is to create some sort of harmony between the male and female sexual nature, hence creating the perfect ecstatic bliss and unity between couples.

Harmony is a condition of balance between the Yin and Yang elements, the balance of positive and negative energy, of light and dark properties, of inward and outward directedness. What a beautiful experience if the man and woman is able to communicate and combine their differences to bring about harmony.

But there are some interferences that blocks the harmonic bliss of a couple. Through a series of tantric techniques and exercises the positive atmosphere of a couple's relationship can be restored. Then how can tantric practices create this sort of harmony? Let us explore some techniques briefly.

One way of creating harmony between the man and woman is through the "Nurturing Meditation". It is a physical form of communication between the couple that must be constantly practised to sustain the love energy in a relationship.

The Nurturing meditation should be practised between the

couple at least twice a day. The goal of this meditation is not for sex, but to create love energy and intimacy. In most cases, couples just want to have sex. They believe that it is only when they are about to have sex that they can explore various parts of the body and assume different positions together to bring about an arousal. Tantric nurturing meditation emphasizes that couples can engage in sexual intimacy without actually having genital contacts. Although couples can end up having sex while engaging in the meditation, but this is not the goal.

To practice the nurturing meditation, the "nurturing position" is required. Many today call it "spooning". In this case, the couple lie together side by side in a spoon like way, cradling against each other. The partner on the inside is engulfed in the arms of the one on the outside. In most cases the partner that feels the most "stressed" or emotionally down (could be either the man or woman) is the one that should assume the inside position. Whether it is evident or not, the aim of the nurturing position is to create some sort of balance necessary for the couple's harmony. When both partners align together, spooning each other, they start vibrating on the same frequently. They become attuned to each other's body. As the partners lie together they should close their eyes and try to relax. By relaxing they have to shut their minds to all other things and concentrate only on the presence of their partner, on the fact that they are lying side by side together. As this continues, both partners must become aware of each other's breath. No words should be said, only the sound of their breaths heard.

Two breathing techniques are used while assuming this position to heighten the effectiveness of this meditation. The first is called the "harmonizing breath". It is used in the first few minutes of lying together. The harmonizing breath emphasizes that the couple's breath must be at the same rhythm. They must inhale together, hold their breath together, exhale together and hold out their breaths together. This is very soothing right?

In the harmonizing breath the partner on the outside is the giver, the one initiating the breath. While the one on the inside is the receiver, the receptive body, the one absorbing the soothing energy that their breaths create into his/her chakra. (The chakra can be assumed as the organ of the energetic or subtle body, which is considered to be distinct and independent from the outward physical body. Chakras are simply the sensitive parts of the body that stimulates sexual energy or leads to arousal).

The second technique is more soothing to both partners. It is done after a few minutes of practicing the harmonizing breath. The second technique is called the " Reciprocal charge breath". In this technique, as one partner breathes in, the other breathes out. In this case, as one partner is holding the breath in, the other would be holding it out. Very stimulating and arousing right?

In this technique, each partner must be consciously aware of the energy he/she is imparting into the other, as well as the one the other partner is giving back. The nurturing meditation produces communication for couples on three levels. On the skin to skin level (the conscious level), on the breath to breath level (subtle respiratory) and then the chakra to chakra level (on a subtler arousing level).

Definitely these levels of communication create some kind of refreshing love energy between the partners. This kind of meditation provides each partner with a charged energy. When this practice is done daily, couples relationships becomes stronger and more intimate. The love then flows from within them and this positively affects their activities for the day.

The Nurturing meditation cannot be complete until the couple look into one another's eyes after practicing the breathing technique. They don't have to say anything to each other but to just stare upon each other's face. Both partners would notice the light of love that would radiate from their eyes and around them.

To add to the nurturing meditation, couples could also do some sort of yoga meditation together. This is called the meeting of the minds. They both sit facing each other and meditate by focusing the mind on each other.

These things are keys to achieving "Practical harmony" between couples.

The nurturing meditation is an important method that helps couples achieve harmony in their marriage. The partners must also learn to work as a team in so many other ways. Rules that guide their relationship must be set between them. Not "stringent rules", but rules that are created from a mutual understanding of how the partners truly want their relationship to be.

In order for the couple to preserve that kind of understanding, there must be communication and sharing on a very intimate level. Both partners must learn how to do things together. These things include taking a jog together, cooking together, reading together and taking very long walks together. It may even entail meditating together (as have been previously mentioned). Couples should learn to share their deepest fears, thoughts, beliefs etc. All these things are crucial for the survival of the relationship.

Conscious harmony through this practical way of "

Nurturing meditation " is one very effective way of keeping the love and unity together. The goal is to keep both partners constantly "in touch" with each other. Let's take a look at the other options of harmonic practices/meditation you can engage in with your partner.

EFFECTIVE COUPLE'S COMMUNICATION; RECONCILING THE DIFFERENCES (II)

Yes, practical steps like the nurturing meditation is very effective for keeping the harmony and love energy between couples, but is this enough?

You can try every single tantra technique that has ever existed, but if you do not know how to communicate with your partner then the relationship is as good as dead. Sometimes, our partners might do something wrong to us, but if one does not know how to control his/her feelings and pick the right words to say, one might end up hurting his/her partner with words. And it is believed that words have a very lasting effect on people than actions, right?

You see, conscious loving requires conscious

communication. One has to be aware of what he or she is saying. Yes, no matter what if you feel hurt, sad, angry or insecure, you have to communicate this feeling with your partner, but in a very careful and diplomatic manner. Never blame your partner for how you feel.

Although it is quite true that we are less conscious with our actions when we are with the people we love the most. By feeling so comfortable with one's partner, we tend to say whatever comes to mind without critically analyzing it. Most people believe that with the person that you truly love "you don't have to watch your every word, just say it as it comes". But some people don't also understand that as a result of the unchecked words we say, all in the name of being free with the partner, people end up causing disharmony in their relationship.

Yes, we sometimes lose our touch and go out of place with our partner. As we are all humans we are bound to get into disagreements and arguments with our partners. Infact tantra subscribes to the view that because we are all prone to change, external factors as well as differences in the sexual nature, it is perfectly normal for couples to experience disagreements. When one experiences disharmony through confrontation with the partner there is this fueling rage in the inside that could burst out anytime and lead to violence between couples.

On a practical aspect after a couple finds themselves in a heated argument, a partner goes outside to take a walk. In doing so, the burning rate should simmer down. Although most partners try all sorts of vices just to calm down the rage, but then, there is nothing compared to letting go of the argument as soon as possible. It is not by containing the rage by trying to avoid a confrontation with your partner. No, this could be very dangerous at the end. The first practical step is to let your feelings known to your partner. You could still feel angry but be conscious of the use of your words. After doing this just let go as soon as possible. Remember that you love your partner so let love be the first consideration you make before engaging in a confrontation with your partner. Nothing comes out of verbal expression of opposition. It has no cure. Know that it can't solve the problem, so let it go. What is the nature of disharmony, bad communication right?

Before we delve into how bad communication leads to disharmony, let us quickly look into the concept of "Duality". According to tantra, duality is simply one partner thinking and communicating " logically" and the other "emotionally". Our emotions can get the best of us to the point that we will fail to see things from a logical point of view. Now talking about point of view, partners always have their " perspective of things", their own different explanations for what happened. In the concept of duality, while one partner tries to justify himself or herself using a logical point of view, the other partner lets his/her feelings gets in the way of logical reasoning. Both partners as a result of the concept of duality speaks in two different languages (emotional and logical), whereas neither can get what the other is saying. Both partners feel in the right as a result of their different perspective of seeing things.

At this point, the partner with the logical point of view has to step up and take charge. This is because the emotional partner is ruled by feelings, at that point he or she can't be easily convinced. The only step that the logical person can do is to succumb to the reasoning of the emotional one. The emotional partner is clouded with feeling hurt, insecurities, so he or she needs to be loved, to be held and to be heard. First, the one with the logics has to apologize and remind the partner that at that point they are both not in harmony. Secondly, both partners need to get into the nurturing position and practice the nurturing meditation immediately.

Although, one must admit that in the middle of a fight with the partner, it sounds almost impossible to suggest the "nurturing meditation". However, as tantric sex proposes, one must never forget one of the rules of commitment which is the maintenance of harmony. Although practicing nurturing meditation would not resolve the dispute, however the practice would ensure that they both reach a conscious understanding that they both have to be in harmony, this is the only way the dispute can be settled.

You would find out that as you practice the nurturing meditation a new understanding of the situation comes into view. In the process of meditation, face each other, connect together by looking into each other's eyes, you would then realize that the argument has diminished in importance. But in no case should you talk about your subject of confrontation for that day again. Shift it to the next day, by then neither of you would be under the influence of the bad energy (anger or hurt). In other to have a better neutral understanding of the situation one can even invite a third party. It could be either a trusted counsellor or friend to discuss the subject of confrontation with. A third party can be able to scrutinize the situation properly, and plus many couples tend to pick their words more carefully when a third party is around.

The "No-fault language" is next on the list. In this case both partners acknowledge that their disagreements belong to both of them. They would have to forgive each other and agree that love, forgiveness and mutual harmony has the strength to solve the situation. The nurturing meditation dissolves any fuel of rage in both partners mind. Even if they find themselves going back into that same argument, they should take up the nurturing practice again. This of course balances the energy synchronization between the couples.

But it should be noted that there actually some couples who have battled for long, couples who have grown very apart from each other. It would be very difficult in trying to restore the harmony between these couples that have grown apart from each other. In this case both partners have to acknowledge that the relationship is dead, bury it and move on with their lives. But still, some partners who find themselves in this situation, still have love for themselves.

Apart from the three-step method of restoring harmony explained briefly above, (letting go, reconnecting with the nurturing meditation and using the No-fault language) the gift of love is also another way partners can heal their hurts.

We all have to acknowledge that no matter what, love is the greatest gift of all. So, for many tantric couples who need to restore back harmony, they try to demonstrate their perception of love as a gift by bringing gifts to one another. This serves as a way of appreciating one's partner. It could be something material or immaterial, anything at all to show appreciation to the partner. Most cultures today use flowers as that "gift of love", but it could also be a box of chocolate, a necklace, preparing a lovely meal etc. One can even verbally offer a gift of love by just simply saying " I love you". Those three words can heal any emotional wounds if both partners would allow it, and let go of the confrontation. For tantric practitioners, gifts go a really long way in keeping the harmony. It is like an act of offering. By giving gifts, you are honoring or paying homage to the partner.

Compromise can also be considered as a gift of love. How? This is when you sacrifice your time to your partner's cause even though you would rather be doing something else. Let's say, by taking him/ her to the movies, even though you would rather take a personal time.

Harmony can never be fulfilled if both partners are not conscious of their actions and words towards each other. Tantra practice suggests that these aforementioned techniques in this subtopic should be carefully followed by the tantrican couple in achieving a blissful harmony.

HEALING THE WOUNDS; RECONCILING THE DFFERENCES (III)

It is interesting to note the complications that have arose in contemporary times when it comes to the issue of harmony between couples. It would not be out of line to assert the fact that "sex" heals love in the eras before the modern time. Tantric practices originally from the far east witnessed as early Hindu practitioners of tantric yoga experienced and taught sexual play and its union as an act of joyful celebration. In those times sexual bliss demonstrated connectedness. It showed the symbolic affirmation of the unity of the couple as a pathway to achieving spiritual fulfillment. However, the depths of wounds caused these days by hurtful words, hurtful actions and man's lack of proper connection to the natural world, makes it almost impossible to achieve spiritual sublimity and sexual unity through the healing of psychosexual wounds.

The "age of darkness" is what these modern times have been referred to. This is because many of us have been misguided by a falsehood reality, a reality that is devoid of inner spiritual understanding, thereby blocking one's path to sexual bliss. Our misconceptions about sex in this modern age is a great block to sexual bliss and unity. Our freedom, the art and act of "sex" has been bound to chains by religious laws, parental chastisement and society's judgements. Many people have been made to believe that sex is somewhat an unholy act that cannot be performed just by anybody except in a "certain situation". Even for the married folks that are found in the " certain situation " have been restricted by religion and the society to only some few sexual acts and positions (the missionary position as one of the few accepted sexual positions).

Viewed as an extreme sexual act, some couples have been condemned for practicing oral sex. Many of these sex practices like the oral sex have been placed in people's consciousness as unholy and filthy. Infact, many have the conception that sex is only to be enjoyed for the sake of procreation. All these preconceptions and many more not mentioned here is enough to limit the sexual flow of the couple and block them from attaining the ultimate sexual bliss and healing.

To make this worse the guilt a person might feel because he or she is engaged in sex and thoughts before marriage, or because he/she experienced some sort of unspeakable sexual pleasure is enough to dim the lights of sexual bliss. Not to forget the fact that many view sex as a misfortune, a sort of carrier of disease because of the outbreak and fear of AIDS. Thankfully though, the creation of protectives (like condoms) is a saving grace to the problem and fear of diseases like AIDS. However, this is still not the solution to a sexual bliss, to unleashing the wild god/goddess within us.

Our consciousness and sensitivity about what to do and what not to do about sex, how to do it, when to do it and who to do it with, has a negative effect on our ability to project love and to feel it through the sexual center.

Should our integrity and moral uprightness be determined by our sexual lives?

Despite our acclaimed revolution, in our world today, many are still convinced that "true love" excludes sex and vice versa. All these negativities about sex caused by fallacious sexual assumptions and misinformation is enough to have a negative effect on our present and future sexuality. The application of tantric principles to sexuality can eliminate the deep wounds that are etched by deep fears about sex, it's misconceptions and our sexual hurts. Tantra addresses negativity on a very deep level. It tries to match the Yin and Yang elements (The dark and light factors about sex).

Tantric sex enforces a balancing act on the actual nature of the man and woman. Tantric sex is regarded as a great tool for healing because it not only creates a balance between the Yin and Yang elements, but also creates a balance that can be achieved for the negative sexual histories we bring to a relationship.

The art of healing places its reference in the "chakra system". Tantra suggests that negative imprints from sexual misconceptions and past experiences makes their home in the region of the second chakra, just like how heartbreaks could be attributed to the region of the fourth chakra. To shed positive light to this negative situation, tantra addresses that in order to bring about healing, we have to pay attention on the afflicted chakra. The second chakra (if the tantric texts are properly studied), is the genital area in the body referred to as the water element.

Tantra suggests that the first step to take on a personal sexual healing is to shed light on the second chakra. The second chakra is the source of our sexual blockages, the fear, coldness, the anger, using tantra meditation one can create a light and concentrate on the second chakra. For instance, using a vivid image, imagine that the design of the second chakra (moon colored crescent inside circle mantra) is been painted on a door. Imagine the door opens to a room filled with your personal sexual belongings and its inner philosophies. To make this more effective, one must enter the room with a torched lantern. You must walk past every single belonging in the room, as this aids to overcome personal obstacles regarding the subject of sex and its related issues. The purpose of this meditation is to ensure that one has to critically analyze his/her issues concerning sex activities and pleasures that involves the genital area.

In modern times a therapist or a counselor could be involved to help that person to overcome the sexual fears.

The heart chakra known as the fourth chakra is home to all our emotions regarding sex. The fourth chakra is the seat to our intimacy. It is the center of the renegade energy for men and progressive energy for women. Our sexual energy and passion derive its source of power from our emotions. Once a person is filled with negative sexual imprints in the fourth chakra, a compatible negative atmosphere also finds its way in the second chakra, which translates into difficulty in achieving and expressing sexual intimacy. Both partners have to understand their separate strengths so they can nullify their deficiencies in expressing love and sex.

Through the use of the art, science and ritual of tantric love making one can attain a powerful healing energy enough to cure psychosexual wounds and to open doors for a very blissful relationship that is not devoid of harmony in every aspect of the word.

RELIVING THE TANTRIC SEX MOMENT OVER AND OVER AGAIN.

Tantra has already taught us that in order to achieve "mind blowing sex" and to keep the love energy between partners, they must learn the art of "conscious love". Everything has to be consciously done because no love is self-sustainable (as has been previously mentioned). However, along the lines of being eager to keep the love energy flowing, many couples still end up losing their touch. Yes, tantra offers various interesting techniques of extreme and beautiful love making, however after a very long time and years of extreme sexual bliss, a couple might end up falling into a period of boredom.

A couple might even still end up having " tantric sex " till the end of their days, but this is because it becomes an established routine after a long time of "love affair" between the couples. Frankly, they may grow weary again, so how can they light the torch of spontaneous love making again?

Subtopics in this chapter have dealt with the nurturing meditation as being a good startup for igniting the love energy between partners. However, to perform the act of love making, a sort of premeditation, a mental preparation for love has to be laid down. Mental preparation for love making is a very important ritual for the tantric partners before they begin their sexual activities. Firstly, it involves

185

setting the mind away from the stress of external factors. Using and preparing for all sorts of meditation (tantric), both partners have to forget about their problems, their differences and tune their minds to each other. The bedroom is mostly regarded as a "sacred groom" for married couples, so it should be kept that way.

They should beautify their bedroom with all sorts of arts, decorating of with beautiful crystals, sheets, draperies, colors and designs. Many assume foreplay to be touching various and sensitive parts of your partner's body, but this should not be it's only definition. Foreplay could also be taking a bath for the preparation of love making. The bath should be regarded as a rite, a purification that washes away the cares of the day and cleanses the energetic physical body in preparation of a spiritual union with one's partner. After the bath, one can apply oil and lotion for easy stimulation. But one should be careful not to use deodorant in this sort of preparation because it represses and restricts the body's natural erotic perfumes.

After applying lotions and oil both partners should put on attractive wears (I.e. the female putting on a sexy lingerie) that would add fuel to the sexual energy of both partners. After all this mental preparation/foreplay is made, then the love making games can begin.

Before you and your loved one start the real deal in the sex, both of you would be anticipating to peel off your clothes from each other. This is why attractive wears is crucial for mental preparation. A wonderful way to begin the process is to lie atop of each other while still clothed and gaze deeply into each other's eyes. Gazing into each other's eyes increases the intimacy between you and your partner. After doing this, both you and your partner should fall into the breathing technique, as has been previously explained in a subtopic in this chapter. After this episode, both partners can begin the process starting with kissing each other. Even while kissing, both partners should still maintain eye contact as it is very fundamental to enjoying tantric sex. As you both kissing each other, things would start falling into place.

Tantra suggests that the process of love making should not be rushed into, both partners have to slow down and take their time in every part of the body they touch. Remember, the foreplay should take a great deal and effort in lasting longer than the engaging of the genital contact itself. The purpose of a lasting foreplay is to build up the sexual energy between both partners. Even in the process of love making both partners must still slow down. This message is particularly for the man. He should learn to thrust slowly to create a more sensual experience. Positions also determine a lot in tantric sex. Infact instead of thrusting, the man could penetrate his partner while she sits on him, swaying gently while in this position. As more energy builds, both partners should start rocking back and forth before the man finally starts thrusting.

Hmmm...here is one interesting part to always keep in mind. Both partners must learn to stop the orgasm in sex. How? As you and your partner start to feel yourself climaxing just stop the impending orgasm. Once it has been stopped, resume your sexual acts until orgasm approaches again. Both of you should keep stopping yourself to reach orgasm until you can no longer control it again. BAM!!!you both create for yourselves a mind blowing stored-in orgasm.

Remember, a great deal of time has to be set aside for tantric sex. This is necessary for both partners if they want to explore various tantric sex techniques.

CONCLUSION

The subject of love is indeed a very sensitive one. It is very simple, fun and benefitting to be in love. But as simple and fun falling in love appears to be, there are some essential ingredients in finding it and keeping it. The path to finding love starts from when we are single. This chapter has earlier emphasized on the fact that the key to falling in love with someone else is to first falling in love with yourself. You need to project enough confidence in yourself, so you can find yourself in a peaceful relationship, devoid of insecurities.

As the chapter proceeds, we talked about what it really meant to fall in love and how to spot the perfect love partner for you.

A session was also prepared for just the married folks. Techniques that would help in constantly sustaining the love energy between couples were also discussed. Key themes that helps the Tantric couples and that should always be remembered are as follows;

I. The nurturing meditation should always be practised at least twice a day amongst couples, to keep the love energy together.

ii. Learn to consciously communicate with one another using the No-fault language.

iii. Always remember that even in the middle of an argument with your partner, nothing is more important than restoring the love, harmony and connection as a partner.

iv. Remember that the goal of tantric sex is for a spiritual connection with your partner and not just for physical and genital satisfaction.

Printed in Great Britain
by Amazon

83838493R00113